165608

DWM 2 0 SEP 1976

N   £2·60

796. 4809047

sbn

ABCEFGKPRSWXY   10.11.79

N.N.

OLYMPIC
HANDBOOK

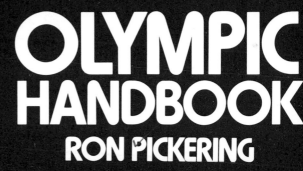

OLYMPIC
HANDBOOK
RON PICKERING

M

Half-title page: The girl who captured the hearts of the public at Munich was diminutive Olga Korbut of the USSR who although she finished only seventh overall took the gold medal on the beam and for the team performance of the superb Soviet team. Title page: Britain's sole gold medallist in track and field athletics in 1972 was Mary Peters from Belfast, who culminated more than 17 years as a club athlete by winning the pentathlon.

The following abbreviations have been used, unless otherwise specified:

Afg - Afghanistan: AHO — Netherlands Antilles; Alb - Albania; Alg - Algeria; Arg - Argentina; ARS - Saudi Arabia; Aus - Australia; Aut - Austria; Bah - Bahamas; Bar - Barbados; Bel - Belgium; Ber - Bermuda; Bir - Burma; Bol - Bolivia; Bra - Brazil; Bul - Bulgaria; CAF - Central Africa; Can - Canada; Cey - Ceylon; Cgo - Congo; Cha - Chad; Chi - Chile; CIV - Ivory Coast; Cmr - Cameroon; COK - Congo Kinshasa; Col - Colombia; Cor - Sth Korea; CRC - Costa Rica; Cub - Cuba; Dah - Dahomey; Den - Denmark; Dom - Dominican Republic; Ecu - Ecuador; Egy - United Arab Republic; Esp - Spain; Eth - Ethiopia; Fij - Fiji; Fin - Finland; Fra - France; Gab - Gabon; GBR - Great Britain; GDR - German Democratic Republic; Ger - German Federal Republic; Gha - Ghana; Gre - Greece; Gua - Guatemala; Gui - Guinea; Guy - Guyana; Hai - Haiti; HBR - British Honduras; HKG - Hong Kong; Hol - Netherlands; Hon - Honduras; Hun - Hungary; Ina - Indonesia; Ind - India; Irl - Ireland; Irn - Iran; Irq - Iraq; Isl - Iceland; Isr - Israel; Ita - Italy; ISV - Virgin Islands; Jam - Jamaica; Jor - Jordan; Jpn - Japan; Ken - Kenya; Khm - Cambodia; Kuw - Kuwait; Lbr - Liberia; Lba - Libya; Les - Lesotho; Lib - Lebanon; Lie - Liechtenstein; Lux - Luxembourg; Mad - Madagascar; Mal - Malaysia; Mar - Morocco; Maw - Malawi; Mex - Mexico; Mgl - Mongolia; Mli - Mali; Mlt - Malta; Mon - Monaco; Nca - Nicaragua; Nep - Nepal; Ngr - Nigeria; Nig - Niger; Nor - Norway; NZL - New Zealand; Pak - Pakistan; Pan - Panama; Par - Paraguay; Per - Peru; Phi - Philippines; Pol - Poland; Por - Portugal; PRK - Nth Korea; Pur - Puerto Rico; ROC - Rep. of China; Rom - Rumania; SA - South Africa; Sal - El Salvador; Sen - Senegal; Sin - Singapore; SLE - Sierra Leone; SMR - San Marino; Som - Somali Republic; Sud - Sudan; Sui - Switzerland; Sur - Surinam; Swe - Sweden; Swz - Swaziland; Syr - Syria; Tai - Taiwan; Tan - Tanzania; Tch - Czechoslovakia; Tha - Thailand; Tog - Togo; Tri - Trinidad and Tobago; Tun - Tunisia; Tur - Turkey; Uga - Uganda; URS - USSR; Uru - Uruguay; USA - United States; Ven - Venezuela; VNM - Viet Nam; Vol - Upper Volta; Yug - Yugoslavia; Zai - Zaire; Zam - Zambia.

Records specified as fully automatic or electric have been included for interest: both hand and automatic timing are used (and must be used together in events up to 400m), and the hand timing is normally used to give the official result. The World Rankings in athletics for 1975 have been ratified by the International Amateur Athletics Federation; the World Rankings for swimming have been ratified by the Fédération Internationale de Natation Amateur.

Acknowledgements

The publishers are grateful to Tony Duffy for supplying all the illustrations.

© Ron Pickering 1976

ISBN 0 333 19397 0

Second Impression, 1976

First published in 1976 by
Macmillan London Limited
London and Basingstoke
Associated companies in New York,
Dublin, Melbourne, Johannesburg and Delhi

First published in Canada
in 1976 by the
Macmillan Company of Canada Ltd.
70 Bond Street
Toronto, Ontario
M5B 1X3

Filmset by Yaleset Ltd, London SE25
Printed in Great Britain by Chapel River Press, Andover

Contents

INTRODUCTION

Despite mounting political, social and economic pressures the Olympic Festival revived by Baron Pierre de Coubertin survives — albeit with interruptions for world confrontations and such ghastly interventions as the massacre of the Israeli athletes in Munich. If this prompts the question, 'Why should it survive?' I can do no better than to quote the International Olympic Committee, when faced with political intrusions in 1956: 'In an imperfect world international competitions would never be held if participation in sports events were cancelled whenever human rights were violated.' Not only do the Games survive, but every four years they produce the greatest sporting spectacle in the world. They provide a challenge to the youth of the world to preserve the ideals of amateur sport, which are based on the ethic of fair play.

In Munich more than 10,000 athletes representing 123 countries competed for 195 Olympic titles, yet such was the standard that 75 countries received no medals whatsoever. For every one athlete taking part there were 100,000 followers around the world reading, listening or viewing. From Montreal the media will carry the Games to one billion people.

Montreal has learned much from Munich and already has its own hard-earned lessons to pass on. Faced with spiralling inflation and labour problems the Olympic organizers are fighting a desperate race against time to complete the competition sites. We can only wish Montreal well in their efforts to stage Canada's first Olympic Games.

This will be my sixth Games and for me there is simply nothing else in the world of sport that can capture and sustain the electrically charged atmosphere that is created by the Olympics even before the opening ceremony. My job as a writer and a television commentator is to link the viewer with that excitement — whether the event is track and field, gymnastics or weight-lifting.

This book is a modest attempt to set the scene for Olympic enthusiasts. It is an armchair guide, recalling past endeavours and attempting to predict Montreal winners from an assessment of current performances. It has certainly not been done in isolation — Tony Duffy has produced a unique collection of pictures, and I have also called on several of my colleagues from both coaching and broadcasting to help with the expertise. For all of us it meant sticking our necks out, but if sport were easy to predict it would lose its excitement. We won't mind being wrong as long as you, the readers, enjoy the '76 Montreal Olympics.

FROM ATHENS TO MUNICH

Athens 1896 In 1889 a French nobleman, Baron Pierre de Coubertin, was commissioned by the French Government to study physical education and culture in the civilized world; he came up with the idea of reviving the ancient Greek Olympic Games. He envisaged that the Games would be held in Paris but the Greeks insisted on Athens when the original site of Olympia proved unsatisfactory. A new stadium was built, but the 233-yard track was totally unsatisfactory; it was an awkward shape with very tight bends and a loose surface. Twelve countries were represented and competitors and officials numbered only 260, while in Munich the total was 10,123. In 1896, tremendous crowds of up to 80,000 watched the US dominate the track and field, and the Germans the gymnastics. Edwin Flack of Australia became the first double gold medallist, winning the 800 and 1500 metre races, and Spiridon Louis won Greece's only gold medal in the marathon.

Paris 1900 Conceived by the French, the second 'revived' Games were put on as a side show to the great Paris Exhibition. The facilities were widely dispersed and the track and field events were held on grass. The US again dominated the track and field, taking 17 out of 23 gold medals. Canadian George Orton was gold medallist in the 3,000 metre steeplechase. Great Britain won the 800, 1,500 and 4,000 metre steeplechase, but the supreme athlete of the Games was Alvin Kraenzlein of the US whose total of four individual gold medals in track and field has never been equalled. Fred Lane began a swimming tradition for Australia when he won the 200 metre freestyle. The marathon again provided a home win with Michael Theato but the Games were severely criticized because they were spread over five months.

St Louis 1904 Again the Games were a side show to the World Fair. Facilities at Washington University were crude and because of the cost of travel only eight countries outside North America attended. The biggest attendance was a mere 2,000 spectators. The track was three laps to a mile and US athletes broke almost every Olympic record. They also produced three triple champions. Canada had four gold medallists, including Montreal policeman Emile Desmarteau, who became Canada's first Olympic champion when he won the 56lb weight throw.

London 1908 Following the debacle of St Louis, London rescued the Games from becoming a permanent side show and for the first time managed to put them on a truly international basis. A major stadium was created at White City which was three laps to a mile, surrounded

by a banked concrete cycle track and enclosing a swimming pool which was 100 metres long! Although the Games were a model for future organization, there was much dissent among the twenty nations who participated. In particular there was great enmity between Great Britain and the USA. The US participants refused to dip their flag to the King and two of the four hundred metre runners refused to take part in a re-run following an incident in which one Carpenter was said to have impeded Wyndham Halswell, a London Scot. Halswell then had to run over for the gold medal on his own, making a travesty of the final. Later, the collapse and disqualification of Dorando Pietri in the marathon also remained a controversial issue for years to come, with few remembering the name of the winner, Hayes of the US. The 1908 Games are also remembered as those which fixed the distance of the present marathon. It was planned to run from Windsor to Shepherds Bush, which was exactly 26 miles, but a further 365 yards were added so that the finish line was in front of the Royal Box! The number of sports was expanded to 20 and Great Britain made a clean sweep in yachting, lawn tennis, rowing, polo and racquets! Canada made an excellent showing and won 13 medals, including four gold.

Stockholm 1912 Following de Coubertin's appeal for a more dignified Games, Sweden produced a 'classic' with superb athletic performances. Football, modern pentathlon, game shooting, and equestrianism were added and gold medals were presented for architecture, painting, sculpture, music, literature and mountain climbing! Thus the cultural Olympic Games were born. The remarkable North American Indian Jim Thorpe of the US won both the decathlon and pentathlon with enormous margins to spare. Later there was great sadness when he had to hand his medals back after admitting that he had been paid as a baseball player in a minor league. Another great hero of these Games was the first of the 'flying Finns', Hannes Kilehmainen, who won the 5,000 and 10,000 metre races and the 8,000 metre cross-country event. The Pacific produced its first champion in Duke Paca Kahanamoku of Hawaii, who won the 100 metre freestyle event in swimming.

Antwerp 1920 The Games were resumed in Antwerp but were sadly bruised and battered by recent war and revolution. The defeated nations were expelled and the Soviet Union remained absent until 1952. The Olympic flag and oath were introduced. It was the beginning of the era of runner Paavo Nurmi of Finland. Canadian

boxers did well, winning five of Canada's eight medals. Britain's Jack Beresford had been wounded in Flanders yet only narrowly lost the single skulls to John B Kelly of the US, later known as the father of Grace Kelly, now Princess Grace of Monaco. Beresford went on to win the single skulls in 1924 and established his reputation as Britain's greatest oarsman. Albert Hill was another who had fought in France; at the age of 35 he ran seven races in eight days, winning the 800 metres and 1,500 metre events, and finishing second in the 3,000 metre team race. Hannes Kilehmainen won the marathon to add to his gold medals of eight years earlier.

Paris 1924 An enormous increase in the scale of the Games took place in Paris when 44 countries entered some 5,533 competitors. A 500 metre track was built accommodating 60,000 spectators. It was the era of the peerless Paavo Nurmi of Finland who had earlier won three gold medals and a silver in track events at Antwerp. Unbeaten in any race between the two Games, he began collecting his unsurpassed 22 ratified world records. In Paris he won four more gold medals, making his Olympic tally nine gold and three silver. Britain produced their only 100 metre champion in Harold Abrahams; Eric Liddell of Scotland won the 400 metre event and Douglas Lowe won the first of his two gold medals at 800 metres. Johnny Weissmuller of

9

the US, who later became most famous of all film Tarzans, collected the first three of his total of five gold medals in swimming.

Amsterdam 1928 For the first time, women were allowed to compete in track and field events and in gymnastics. The women's high jump was won by Canadian Ethel Catherwood, who became known as 'Saskatoon Lily'. Her win set a world record at 1.59 metres. Canada's Percy Williams won both the 100 metre and 200 metre sprints, and Great Britain's Lord Burghley won the 400 metre hurdles. India began its domination of field hockey and Haiti won its only gold medal to date. The track was 400 metres long, pigeons were released for the first time and the introduction of scoreboards and loud-speakers gave the best communications so far.

Los Angeles 1932 A massive new 105,000 seat stadium was packed for the opening ceremony. An Olympic village was introduced, and was patrolled by cowboys on horseback! Thirty-seven countries were involved but there was only a small entry from Europe because of the expense of travel. The US began to dominate the sprints and jumps but Britain upheld her middle distance traditions for the fourth successive Games with Tommy Hampson's victory and world record in the 800 metres (1:49.7). Duncan McNaughton of Canada won the high jump and Henry Pearce of Australia retained his single sculls title;

the outstanding woman athlete was the immortal Mildred 'Babe' Didrikson of the US.

Berlin 1936 An attempt was made by the Germans to use the Games for propaganda but a magnificent stadium and good organization produced superb athletic performances. The torch ceremony was introduced. The legendary athlete from Berlin was Jesse Owens of the US—the greatest sprinter and jumper ever. He won four gold medals and equalled or broke 12 Olympic records. The Japanese marathon runners excelled, as did the Dutch women swimmers. While Germany dominated the equestrian events, rowing and gymnastics, Jack Lovelock of New Zealand won the long-talked-about 1,500 metre event in track. Canadian Francis Amyot won the gold medal in the 1,000 metre Canadian singles canoeing event.

London 1948 The war robbed both Tokyo and Helsinki of awarded Games but London picked up the pieces on a very limited budget. There were 4,106 competitors from 59 countries. Fanny Blankers-Koen of the Netherlands was the outstanding athlete of the Games, winning four gold medals, and 17-year-old Bob Mathias of the US won the decathlon.

Helsinki 1952 The smallest nation staged the biggest and best Games so far with over 5,000 competitors from 69 countries, including the USSR who re-appeared after an absence of 40 years. The great Zatopek of Czechoslovakia won the 5,000 and 10,000 metre events and the marathon, which he ran for the first time. His wife Dana won the javelin. The Australian girls won both the sprints (Marjorie Jackson) and the 80 metre hurdles (Shirley Strickland). With no gold medals, Helsinki was regarded as a disaster for Great Britain. Canadians brought home one gold and two silver medals.

Melbourne 1956 The first-ever Games in the Southern Hemisphere took place in the famous Oval cricket ground but entries were reduced because many athletes were 'out of season'. Strict quarantine regulations meant that the equestrian events were held in Stockholm. Bobby Morrow of the US took three sprint gold medals and the Russian sailor, Vladimir Kuts, won both the 5,000 and 10,000 metres. Britain's first winner on the track since 1932 was Chris Brasher in the steeplechase. The Australian girls continued their dominance of the sprints and the darling of the home crowd was Betty Cuthbert, who won three gold medals. Romance split the iron curtain when Hal Connelly, the US winner of the hammer, became engaged to and later married Olga Fikotova, the Czechoslovakian winner of the discus.

Rome 1960 There were 84 nations with 6,000 competitors; in spite of very hot conditions Rome created a perfect setting of the finest Games to date. Medals were widely spread for the first time. Wilma Rudolf of the US won three sprint medals and Africa won its first gold medal when Abebe Bikila of Ethiopia came first in the marathon. Herb Elliott of Australia ran away with the 1,500 metre race in a new world record. Don Thompson maintained Britain's great walking tradition in the longest race of the Games, the 50 kilometre walk. Australian swimmers excelled and Murray Rose and Dawn Fraser became household names.

Tokyo 1964 Meticulously planned, the Tokyo Games had excellent but very costly facilities. There were four British golds from Mary Rand (long jump), Anne Packer (800 metres), Lynn Davies (long jump) and Ken Matthews (20km walk). Al Oerter of the US collected his third consecutive gold medal in the discus and Peter Snell of New Zealand retained his 800 metre crown and went on to win the 1,500 metres. Don Schollander matched Johnny Weissmuller's record of five swimming golds and Dawn Fraser of Australia won her fourth Olympic gold, which included three successive wins in the 100 metres freestyle.

Mexico 1968 Mexico's altitude of over 7,000 feet brought a new dimension to athletics. It affected all endurance events badly, but improved explosive events like the sprints and long jump. Bob Beamon of the US made a phenomenal leap of 29ft 2in in the long jump—more than two feet beyond the Olympic record. Oerter triumphed yet again in the discus for an all-time record of four successive golds. Africa won every distance race over 800 metres. Vera Caslavska of Czechoslovakia brought her gold tally in gymnastics to seven. Dick Fosbury of the US introduced his 'flop' and Great Britain's David Hemery won the 400 metre hurdles, shattering the world record by 0.7 seconds. Canada won a gold medal on the last day of competition, when the equestrian team won the Prix des Nations jumping event.

MUNICH SUPERSTARS

The chilling juxtaposition of political terrorism with high athletic endeavour makes one wonder how long the ideals and spirit of Baron Pierre de Coubertin's modern Olympic movement can survive. It is threatened not only by political intervention but by a whole gamut of social, commercial, professional and medical malpractice that is corrupting the very essence of the Games. It may be that the Games will always be exploited by those who see them as a chance for publicity, but I believe they still represent the greatest gathering of sportsmen and women in the world, the vast majority of whom believe in and cherish those ideals which gave rise to the first Olympic Games. For those of us who are professionally involved with the Games, it is now our responsibility to consider the athletic achievements in Munich as we approach the 1976 Games in Montreal with high hopes and renewed optimism.

If one can isolate the performances at the Munich Games from other events, one quickly realizes that records were broken at every turn. While one may marvel at men of the calibre of Mark Spitz, Valeriy Borzov, Lasse Viren and Kip Keino, a closer look at these Games reveals that they really belonged to the women. In swimming they broke the Olympic record in every event and the world record in all but two events. They almost matched 'Mark the Shark' with 15-year-old Shane Gould who won three gold medals, each with new world records, plus a silver and a bronze medal. In athletics the story was much the same, with only two Olympic records surviving; the women captured many of their medals so dramatically that they held the crowds spellbound.

One incredible rise to fame was that of 16-year-old high jumper Ulrike Meyfarth of West Germany. She finished third in her own national championships, only just making the team for Munich. Her lifetime best high jump was 1.85 metres (6ft 0¾in), which is her own standing height. Yet in the Games this schoolgirl fought a four and a half hour battle to win the gold medal, equalled the world record of 1.92 metres (6ft 3½in) and had three near misses at a new world record of 1.93 metres (6ft 4½in).

Despite Ulrike's marvellous victory, probably the best known woman athlete in Germany is Heide Marie Rosendahl. She brought her Olympic career to its height when she won the long jump, finished second in the pentathlon, and probably most memorable of all, gained a second gold medal in the 4 x 100 metres relay by holding off the powerful East German girl, Renate Stecher, who had earlier won both

Above: Ludmila Bragina of the USSR, the champion
of the 1,500m in Munich who broke the world record in
the heat, the semi-final and the final. Above right:
Heide Rosendahl (left) of West Germany closed a
brilliant career in track and field by winning gold medals
at the long jump, and 4 x 100m relay and a silver medal in
the pentathlon. Below right: Mark 'the Shark' Spitz set
a unique record in Munich when he captured seven gold
medals in swimming.

Below: The superb resurgence of Finnish
track superiority at Munich was demonstrated
not only by Lasse Viren (who won the 5,000
and 10,000m events) but also by Pekka
Vasala, seen here winning the 1,500m.

the 100 and 200 metre sprints. In the 1968 Olympic games, Heide had
lost an almost certain gold medal through injury, and then a year later
at the European Championships in Athens was robbed of two other
gold medals when the West German team withdrew for political
reasons. So Munich provided the ideal setting for victory in front of
her own home crowd.

Ludmila Bragina, the extraordinary Soviet star, not only won the
1,500 metres but smashed the world record three times during the
Games on her way to victory. It was the most uncompromising piece
of running in Munich and in bringing the world record to within a frac-
tion of 4 minutes, Ludmila brought a new dimension to the toughest
event in the women's athletic calendar.

Mary Peters of Belfast won Britain's only gold medal in track and
field when she smashed the world record for the pentathlon. She had
an enormous following and was one of the most popular champions in
Munich.

Another impressive display by women athletes at Munich was put

on by the gymnasts, in response to the demands of their judges that they should concentrate on being essentially feminine in dress, in hair styles and in the quality of their movement. They were warned that if they copied the men in their strength-dominated form of gymnastics, they would lose marks. None responded better than the elfin-like, pert and vivacious 17-year-old Olga Korbut, or the delightfully graceful 18-year-old Ludmilla Turischeva.

The Munich Games were a great victory for women not only in terms of technical achievement but also in terms of sportsmanship, in which they were often unmatched by the men. The memory of their performances raises the pulse rate as we contemplate the Montreal Games of 1976.

TIMETABLE OF EVENTS

Sports	Sat. July 17	Sun. July 18	Mon. July 19	Tues. July 20	Wed. July 21	Thu. July 22	Fri. July 23	Sat. July 24	Sun. July 25	Mon. July 26	Tues. July 27	Wed. July 28	Thu. July 29	Fri. July 30	Sat. July 31	Sun. Aug. 1
Opening ceremonies	●															
Archery											●	●	●	○		
Athletics							●	●	●	●		●	●	○	●	
Basketball		●	●	●	●	●	●	●	●	●	●					
Boxing		●	●	●	●	●	●	●	●	●				○	●	
Canoeing												●	●	○	●	
Cycling		●		●	●	●		●		●						
Equestrian Sports						●	●	●	●		●	●	●			●
Fencing				●	●	●	●	●	●	●	●	●	●			
Football		●	●	●		●	●	●	●		●	●	●		●	
Gymnastics		●	●	●	●	●	○									
Handball		●	●	●		●	●	●		●	●	●				
Hockey		●	●	●	●	●	●	●	●			●	●	○		
Judo										●	●	●	●	○	●	
Modern Pentathlon		●	●		●	●										
Rowing		●	●	●	●	●	●	●	●							
Shooting		●	●	●	●	●	●	●								
Swimming		●	●	●	●	●	●	●	●	●	●					
Volleyball		●	●	●	●	●	●	●	●	●	●		●	○		
Weightlifting		●	●	●	●	●	●	●	●	●	●					
Wrestling				●	●	●	●	●			●	●	●		●	
Yachting			●	●	●	●		●		●	●					
Closing ceremonies																●

20

Timetable of Track and Field Finals

	Fri July 23	Sat July 24	Sun July 25	Mon July 26	Tues July 27	Wed July 28	Thurs July 29	Fri July 30	Sat July 31
MEN	20km walk	100m shot put	800m 400m hurdles discus	200m 10,000m pole vault javelin	Rest Day	110m hurdles 3,000m hammer	400m long jump	5,000m triple jump decathlon	1,500m 4 x 100m 4 x 400m marathon high jump
WOMEN	long jump	javelin	100m	800m pentathlon		200m high jump	400m 100m hurdles discus	1,500m	4 x 100m 4 x 400m shot put

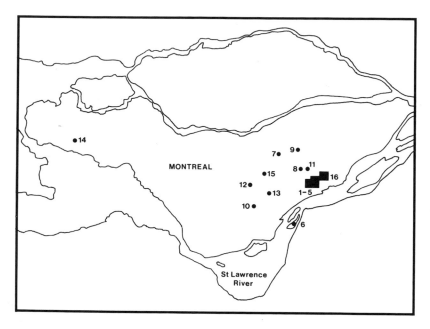

MAP OF MAIN OLYMPIC SITE

1. Olympic Stadium
2. Olympic Pool
3. Olympic Velodrome
4. Maurice Richard Arena
5. Maisonneuve Sports Centre
6. Olympic Basin and site of
    Expo 67
7. Claude Robillard Centre
8. Étienne Desmarteau Centre

9. St Michel Arena
10. Forum
11. Paul Sauvé Centre
12. Winter Stadium
    University of Montreal
13. Molson Stadium
    McGill University
14. Fairview Circuit
15. Mount Royal Circuit
16. Olympic Village

THE CITY OF MONTREAL

The Games are awarded to cities, not to countries, and this year's host is Montreal—one of the oldest and largest cities in Canada. The present population is approaching 2.75 million and although it is a truly cosmopolitan city, the style, cuisine, and flavour of Montreal are very French.

The organizing committee of the Games is called COJO (Comité Organisateur des Jeux Olympiques) and the mascot for the Games is the industrious Canadian beaver, named 'Amik' from the Algonquin Indian word for beaver. The stylized black beaver appearing on the Olympic Games posters wears a red band to symbolize the ribbons which will hold the winners' medals at the Games.

The award of the 1976 Games was made before the present catastrophic world-wide inflation and the original cost estimate of $300 million has risen to over $1,000 million. This, together with serious labour problems, has created great difficulties in the construction of the Olympic Stadium and Swimming Pool; the organizers are now racing against time to complete the construction before 17 July, when the Olympics will be opened by Queen Elizabeth II.

1. SPRINTERS

Sprinting, which involves all races up to and including 400 metres, provides eight thrilling finals in the Games, but the glamour is reserved for the shortest dash—the 100 metres. It is one of the few 'absolute' tests to determine the fastest man or woman in the world. Title holders like Jesse Owens and Valeriy Borzov have become household names, especially when they have emphasized their supremacy by winning the 'double'—the 200 metres. This double victory has now been achieved by seven men and five women. It is interesting to note that both champions in Munich, Valeriy Borzov of the USSR and Renate Stecher of East Germany, had that distinction. They should start favourites to defend their titles in Montreal.

What makes a great sprinter? Coaches argue that sprinters are 'born', not made. They must have an innate ability to run fast, although they can improve with training. Physiques differ widely—from the cruiserweight frame of Bob Hayes (USA) to the elegant linearity of Steve Williams, also of the US, who is the current world record holder for the 100 metres sprint. Renate Stecher's build is very different from that of Irena Szewinska of Poland, but each has the muscular power needed to drive her bodyweight at great speed.

Since the span of time which determines the fastest man or woman is a mere 10 or 11 seconds, each must be capable of a fast start. This is where the discipline of the event is all-important. The tension at the

Left: Two of the leading sprinters are Steve Williams (left), USA, and Don Quarrie (right), Jamaica; but they will have to do battle with Silvio Leonard of Cuba and defending champion Valeriy Borzov of the USSR.

100 METRES (Men)

Munich 1972		*World Rankings 1975*		
1. V. Borzov (URS)	10.14	S. Williams (USA)	9.8w	(9.9)
2. R. Taylor (USA)	10.24	H. Crawford (Tri)	9.8w	(10.0)
3. L. Miller (Jam)	10.33	S. Leonard (Cub)	9.9	
4. A. Korneliuk (URS)	10.36	R. Jones (USA)	9.9	
5. M. Fray (Jam)	10.40	C. Joseph (Tri)	9.9w	
6. J. Hirscht (Ger)	10.40	F. Mata (Ven)	9.9w	
7. Z. Nowosz (Pol)	10.46	H. McTear (USA)	10.0	
H. Crawford (Tri) Dnf.		D. Quarrie (Jam)	10.0	
		V. Borzov (URS)	10.0	
Dnf. = did not finish		V. Patinez (Ven)	10.0	
		M. Gulbaran (Ven)	10.0	
		S. Riddick (USA)	10.0	
		C. Wells (USA)	10.0	

	Fully automatic timing:		
	S. Riddick (USA)	10.05w	(10.26)
	S. Williams (USA)	10.08	
	S. Leonard (Cub)	10.15	
	D. Quarrie (Jam)	10.16	
	V. Borzov (URS)	10.16	
	P. Mennea (Ita)	10.20	
	F. Mata (Ven)	10.20	
	P. Ferrer (Pur)	10.21	

w = wind-assisted

100 METRES (Women)

Munich 1972		*World Rankings 1975*		
1. R. Stecher (GDR)	11.07	R. Stecher (GDR)	11.0	
2. R. Boyle (Aus)	11.23	M. Gang (Ger)	11.0w	(11.2)
3. S. Chivas (Cub)	11.24	S. Priebsch (GDR)	11.0w	(11.1)
4. J. Davis (USA)	11.32	A. Lynch (GBR)	11.1	
5. A. Richter (Ger)	11.38	I. Szewinska (Pol)	11.1	
6. A. Annum (Gha)	11.41	A. Richter (Ger)	11.1	
7. B. Ferrell (USA)	11.45	J. Pavlicic (Yug)	11.1	
8. E. Gleskova (Tch)	12.48	I. Helten (Ger)	11.1	

	Fully automatic timing:	
	R. Stecher (GDR)	11.13
	A. Lynch (GBR)	11.16
	I. Szewinska (Pol)	11.23

w = wind-assisted

start is electric and distractions can be fatal. Every physical and mental faculty must be channeled into an instant explosion on the sound of the gun. Anticipations are tolerated only once. The same single-mindedness must be sustained throughout the race; there must

Left: Valeriy Borzov of the Soviet Union (left),
who captured the gold medal in both the
100m and the 200m sprints in Munich.

200 METRES (Men)

Munich 1972		World Rankings 1975	
1. V. Borzov (URS)	20.00	D. Quarrie (Jam)	19.8
2. L. Black (USA)	20.19	S. Williams (USA)	19.8
3. P. Mennea (Ita)	20.30	S. Leonard (Cub)	20.1
4. L. Burton (USA)	20.37	P. Mennea (Ita)	20.1
5. C. Smith (USA)	20.55	W. Collins (USA)	20.1*
6. S. Schenke (GDR)	20.56	L. Brown (USA)	20.1*w
7. M. Jellinghaus (Ger)	20.65	J. Gilkes (Guy)	20.2
8. H-J. Zenk (GDR)	21.05	C. Joseph (Tri)	20.2w
		R. Jones (USA)	20.2*w
		C. Edwards (USA)	20.2*w
		H. Crawford (Tri)	20.2*w

Fully automatic timing:
D. Quarrie (Jam)	20.12
P. Mennea (Ita)	20.23
R. Jones (USA)	20.3*
J. Gilkes (Guy)	20.39

w = wind-assisted
*220 yds time less 0.1

200 METRES (Women)

Munich 1972		World Rankings 1975		
1. R. Stecher (GDR)	22.40	R. Stecher (GDR)	22.4	
2. R. Boyle (Aus)	22.45	I. Szewinska (Pol)	22.4	
3. I. Szewinska (Pol)	22.74	K. Bodendorf (GDR)	22.7	
4. E. Stropahl (GDR)	22.75	D. Maletzki (GDR)	22.8	
5. A. Kroniger (Ger)	22.89	A. Richter (Ger)	22.8w	(22.9)
6. C. Heinich (GDR)	22.89	M. Gang (Ger)	22.8w	
7. A. Annum (Gha)	22.99	E. Streidt (GDR)	22.9	
8. R. Allwood (Jam)	23.11	A. Lynch (GBR)	22.9w	

Fully automatic timing:
R. Stecher (GDR)	22.44
I. Szewinska (Pol)	22.67
C. Cheeseborough (USA)	22.77
P. Jiles (USA)	22.81
K. Bodendorf (GDR)	22.84
E. Streidt (GDR)	22.95

w = wind-assisted

be no over-reaction to fellow competitors. This tough discipline can
be developed only through serious training and experience.

Both Valeriy Borzov and Renate Stecher have proved themselves
over 100 metres and 200 metres at Munich and in international
competition since, and will be very tough to beat. Borzov will be

severely tested by Silvio Leonard of Cuba, the Pan American champion, by Steve Williams and Steve Riddick of the US, and by Don Quarrie of Jamaica and Haseley Crawford of Trinidad. Quarrie's opportunity may come in the 200 metres along with Leonard and Mennea of Italy.

In the women's 100 metres Andrea Lynch of Great Britain has a great chance to bring home a medal and it could be the gold. She has the experience of beating Stecher and on her day is the fastest starter of any woman in the world. However, Australia's Raelene Boyle is also a very strong contender. She has won three silver medals in the past two Games and may swap them for a gold this time. If the 200 metres is one of the choices of the multi-talented Irena Szewinska of Poland, then no one is safe—not even Stecher. In the short relays, a quick look at the ranking lists indicates that the battle will be between

400 METRES (Men)

Munich 1972		World Rankings 1975	
1. V. Matthews (USA)	44.66	R. Ray (USA)	44.45
2. W. Collett (USA)	44.80	A. Juantorena (Cub)	44.80
3. J. Sang (Ken)	44.92	K. Randle (USA)	44.8*
4. C. Asati (Ken)	45.13	D. Jenkins (GBR)	44.93
5. H-R. Schloeske (Ger)	45.31	B. Brown (USA)	44.9*
6. M. Kukkoaho (Fin)	45.49	B. Herrmann (Ger)	45.10
7. K. Honz (Ger)	45.68	M. Sands (Bah)	45.20*
J. Smith (USA) Dnf.		F. Newhouse (USA)	45.22
		S. Vinson (USA)	45.24
		S. Chepkwony (Ken)	45.2
		A. Brydenbach (Bel)	45.25
		R. Taylor (USA)	45.26
		M. Peoples (USA)	45.26

*440 yds time less 0.3

400 METRES (Women)

Munich 1972		World Rankings 1975	
1. M. Zehrt (GDR)	51.08	I. Szewinska (Pol)	50.50
2. R. Wilden (Ger)	51.21	E. Streidt (GDR)	50.53
3. K. Hammond (USA)	51.64	C. Brehmer (GDR)	50.84
4. H. Seidler (GDR)	51.86	B. Rohde (GDR)	50.98
5. M. Fergerson (USA)	51.96	D. Murray (GBR)	51.28
6. C. Rendina (Aus)	51.99	R. Huhne (GDR)	51.40
7. D. Kaesling (GDR)	52.19	K. Kafer (Aut)	51.4
8. G. Balogh (Hun)	52.39	R. Salin (Fin)	51.58
		D. Sapenter (USA)	51.6
		N. Ilyina (URS)	51.6
		J. Yakubowich (Can)	51.62

Right: In 1975 Britain's David Jenkins travelled to the US to steal their 400m title in the AAU championships — a unique feat this century which sets Jenkins up with a good chance to win the gold in Montreal.

East and West Germany for the women and perhaps between Cuba and the US for the men.

In the longer one-lap sprint (400 metres) Irena Szewinska of Poland is the women's world record holder. If she chooses this event she will be challenged by the East Germans, as well as by Donna Murray of Great Britain, European champion Rita Salin (Finland), and Joyce Yakubowich of Canada. In the men's event David Jenkins of Great Britain has a great opportunity for Britain's first gold medal at 400 metres. While the rankings show two men above him, both their times were recorded in the rarified atmosphere of Mexico City, which makes a significant difference. What makes David Jenkins my favourite is his win in the US Championships in 1975. Winning against the tough US competition should put him next in line to win the Olympic title. However, Alberto Juantorena of Cuba will still be tough to beat and the US have Ronnie Ray, Benny Brown, Maurice Peoples, and Kenny Randle (who has previously beaten David Jenkins over 300 metres). The best four men from the US will make a formidable relay team, but West Germany, Kenya and Great Britain must be in the chase and there are no tougher fighters than the British quartet. If David Jenkins gets the success he deserves in the individual 400, then even the US will have to be way out in front on the final leg of the relay if they are to win the gold.

2. HURDLERS

Tall flexible sprinters are best equipped for the demands of the hurdles; these are sprint races with obstacles which have to be cleared with maximum economy. Men's events are the 110 metre hurdles (the high hurdles), and the 400 metre hurdles, which demand extra physical toughness and endurance.

400 METRES HURDLES

Munich 1972		World Rankings 1975	
1. J. Akii-Bua (Uga)	47.82	J. Bolding (USA)	48.4
2. R. Mann (USA)	48.51	A. Pascoe (GBR)	48.59
3. D. Hemery (GBR)	48.52	J. Akii-Bua (Uga)	48.67
4. J. Seymour (USA)	48.64	R. Mann (USA)	48.74
5. R. Schubert (Ger)	49.65	J. King (USA)	49.03
6. E. Gavrilenko (URS)	49.66	J-C. Nallet (Fra)	49.37
7. S. Tziortzis (Gre)	49.66	R. Cassleman (USA)	49.4
8. Y. Zorin (URS)	50.25	F. Nusse (Hol)	49.48
		J. Hewelt (Pol)	49.5
		Y. Gavrilenko (URS)	49.5
		B. Collins (USA)	49.60

Fully automatic timing:
J. Bolding (USA)   48.55

At Olympic level the US has long dominated both the men's hurdles events, losing the titles only twice. Britain's interest has always been in the 400 metre hurdles and in Montreal Alan Pascoe has a great chance to join previous British winners Lord Burghley and David Hemery. In one exhausting pre-Olympic season Pascoe has won 22 out of 23 races, beating all possible contenders. His one defeat came from defending champion John Akii-Bua of Uganda. Alan Pascoe has superb consistency and great strength, but few will deny the unnerving talent of Akii-Bua. Add two very tough US competitors, Jim Bolding and Ralph Mann, and this becomes one of the great races to savour.

In the high hurdles (110 metres) the US hasn't lost or even looked like losing since 1928, when South African Sydney Atkinson won it. However, France's Guy Drut could bring about their downfall at Montreal. Drut heads the world rankings and holds the world record. In 1975 he beat the US contenders, Charles Foster and Jerry Wilson. An outsider who could cause an upset is a very fluent Cuban, Alejandro Casanas.

Below: Guy Drut of France, who is world record holder for the 110m hurdles and could wrest the title from the US for the first time since 1928.

110 METRES HURDLES (Men)

Munich 1972		World Rankings 1975	
1. R. Milburn (USA)	13.24	G. Drut (Fra)	13.0
2. G. Drut (Fra)	13.34	A. Casanas (Cub)	13.2
3. T. Hill (USA)	13.48	C. Foster (USA)	13.2
4. W. Davenport (USA)	13.50	D. Smith (Bah)	13.2w
5. F. Siebeck (GDR)	13.71	M. Wodzynski (Pol)	13.3
6. L. Wodzynski (Pol)	13.72	C. Jackson (USA)	13.3w
7. L. Nadenicek (Tch)	13.76	L. Shipp (USA)	13.4
8. P. Cech (Tch)	13.86	V. Myasnikov (URS)	13.4
		J. Wilson (USA)	13.4
		J. Pusty (Pol)	13.4
		L. Wodzynski (Pol)	13.4

Fully automatic timing:	
G. Drut (Fra)	13.28
J. Wilson (USA)	13.38
C. Foster (USA)	13.43
T. Munkelt (GDR)	13.45
F. Siebeck (GDR)	13.47

w = wind-assisted

Below: Alan Pascoe, the reigning
Commonwealth and European champion at
400m hurdles, has defeated every other
world-class opponent in his preparation for
Montreal and starts favourite for Great
Britain.

Right: Grazina Rabsztyn of Poland was the
first girl to inflict defeat on defending hurdles
champion Annelie Ehrhardt (East Germany) in
4 years and may start favourite in Montreal.

The women's hurdles, run over 100 metres, is an event dominated by the East Germans and the Poles — the Australians have lost their grip since the length of the race was changed from 80 metres. In Montreal, Annelie Ehrhardt of East Germany will be defending her title against Grazina Rabsztyn of Poland, who was recently the first girl to beat her in any major race for four years.

100 METRES HURDLES (Women)

Munich 1972		*World Rankings 1975*	
1. A. Ehrhardt (GDR)	12.59	G. Rabsztyn (Pol)	12.6
2. V. Bufanu (Rom)	12.84	A. Ehrhardt (GDR)	12.8
3. K. Balzer (GDR)	12.90	N. Lebedyeva (URS)	12.8
4. P. Ryan (Aus)	12.98	B. Nowakowska (Pol)	12.9
5. T. Nowak (Pol)	13.17	T. Nowak (Pol)	12.9
6. D. Straszynska (Pol)	13.18	A. Fiedler (GDR)	13.0
7. A. Krumpholz (GDR)	13.27	E. Rot (Isr)	13.0
8. G. Rabsztyn (Pol)	13.44	N. Tkachenko (URS)	13.0

3. MIDDLE DISTANCE RUNNERS

A look at the great middle distance runners of the past leaves one in no doubt that the 800 and 1,500 metres are the blue-ribboned events of the Games. Lowe, Hampson, Whitfield, Lovelock, Snell, Elliott, Keino — men of this calibre will always be the focal point of world interest, and Montreal's middle distance runners will match or even surpass them.

By comparison the women's events are still developing. The fact that more than a dozen women have broken two minutes for 800 metres is an indication of great progress. In the women's 800 metres, Nina Morgunova of the USSR is just ahead of Mariana Suman of Rumania on rankings but Suman has the faster finish. Canada's Yvonne Saunders has made an impressive move up to 800 metres and could win a medal, as could Marie-François Dubois of France. At 1,500 metres Nina Morgunova and Norway's Greta Anderson Waitz are closely matched, but Francie Larrieu of the US is also a very tough competitor.

In the men's 800 metres, the recent European Championships have revealed the shattering acceleration of Luciano Susanji of Yugoslavia and the exciting potential of Britain's Steve Ovett. In the US Rick Wohlhuter has vanquished all opposition and finished as the top track and field athlete in the world. The Commonwealth Games exposed the raw talent of John Kipkurgat of Kenya, and yet at the end of 1975 it was another Kenyan who was at the head of world rankings — Mike Boit. He won 14 out of 16 major races in eight weeks and missed the world record by 1/10th of a second. Contemplate that line-up and you can appreciate why it would be the race of the Games — if it were not for the 1,500 metres!

800 METRES (Men)

Munich 1972		*World Rankings 1975*	
1. D. Wottle (USA)	1:45.9	M. Boit (Ken)	1.43.8
2. E. Arzhanov (URS)	1:45.9	R. Wohlhuter (USA)	1:44.1
3. M. Boit (Ken)	1:46.0	M. Enyeart (USA)	1:44.9
4. F-J. Kemper (Ger)	1:46.5	L. Susanji (Yug)	1:45.2
5. R. Ouko (Ken)	1:46.5	J. Kipkurgat (Ken)	1:45.3
6. A. Carter (GBR)	1:46.6	W. Wulbeck (Ger)	1:45.4
7. A. Kupczyk (Pol)	1:47.1	Van Damme (Bel)	1:45.4
8. D. Fromm (GDR)	1:48.0	M. Gesicki (Pol)	1:45.4
		F. Bayi (Tan)	1:45.5
		B. Dyce (Jam)	1:45.7
		J. Walker (NZL)	1:45.9
		A. Svenson (Swe)	1:45.9

Below: The 800m event invariably produces great races in the Olympic Games; one wonders who can match the vivid acceleration of Luciano Susanji of Yugoslavia (right), the reigning European champion.

800 METRES (Women)

Munich 1972		World Rankings 1975	
1. H. Falck (Ger)	1:58.6	N. Morgunova (URS)	1:59.4
2. N. Sabaite (URS)	1:58.7	M. Suman (Rom)	1:59.7
3. G. Hoffmeister (GDR)	1:59.2	M-F. Dubois (Fra)	1:59.9
4. S. Zlateva (Bul)	1:59.7	Y. Saunders (Can)	2:00.1
5. V. Nikolic (Yug)	2:00.0	L. Tomova (Bul)	2:00.1
6. I. Silai (Rom)	2:00.0	M. Jackson (USA)	2:00.3
7. R. Stirling (GBR)	2:00.2	U. Klapezynski (GDR)	2:00.3
8. A. Hoffman (Can)	2:00.2	J. Cerchlanova (Tch)	2:00.4
		M. Lazer (Hun)	2:00.5
		E.Katolik (Pol)	2:00.6

If the 800 metres attracts the great 'racers', it is the 1,500 which introduces the element of tactics and the need for considered strategy in training as well as in competition. The crowd always loves runners who try to stay in front from the moment of the gun. Men like Elliott and Bedford make the race a test of physical and mental courage as well as ability; Filbert Bayi of Tanzania is another man of this calibre.

His boldness as a front runner is thrilling and few will forget his 1,500 metre victory and world record in Christchurch. Heading the·pack of chasers in that race was big, blond John Walker of New Zealand, who has since come up very strong. The weakness in Bayi's armour is that he has exposed his hand and Walker has toughened himself to meet the challenge. Walker's new-found strength gave him the

1,500 METRES (Men)

Munich 1972		World Rankings 1975	
1. P. Vasala (Fin)	3:36.3	J. Walker (NZL)	3:32.4
2. K. Keino (Ken)	3:36.8	F. Bayi (Tan)	3:35.0
3. R. Dixon (NZL)	3:37.5	R. Wohlhuter (USA)	3:36.4
4. M. Boit (Ken)	3:38.4	T. Wessinghage (Ger)	3:34.4
5. B. Foster (GBR)	3:39.0	K. Hall (Aus)	3:36.6
6. H. Mignon (Bel)	3:39.1	G. Crouch (Aus)	3:36.9
7. P-H. Wellmann (Ger)	3:40.1	F. Malan (SA)	3:37.2
8. V. Pantelei (URS)	3:40.2	E. Bonzet (SA)	3:37.3
9. T. Polhill (NZL)	3:41.8	R. Dixon (NZL)	3:37.4
10. T. Hansen (Den)	3:46.6	M. Ulimov (URS)	3:37.5
		M. Liquori (USA)	3:37.7
		T. Hansen (Den)	3:37.9

confidence to do his own front running, which has lowered the world mile record to an incredible 3:49.4. Both have a tremendous respect for one another and although the honours are very much on Bayi's side in terms of victories, Walker has appeared invincible since they last met. I am convinced that on Saturday, 31 July, at 1700hrs we shall see another 'mile of the century' or its metric equivalent.

1,500 METRES (Women)

Munich 1972		World Rankings 1975	
1. L. Bragina (URS)	4:01.4	N. Morgunova (URS)	4:06.0
2. G. Hoffmeister (GDR)	4:02.8	G. Andersen Waitz (Nor)	4:07.5
3. P. Cacchi (Ita)	4:02.9	T. Kazankina (URS)	4:07.9
4. K. Burneleit (GDR)	4:04.1	W. Strotzer (GDR)	4:08.0
5. S. Carey (GBR)	4:04.8	N. Andrei (Rom)	4:08.4
6. I. Keizer (Hol)	4:05.1	F. Larrieu (USA)	4:08.5
7. T. Pangelova (URS)	4:06.5	M-F. Dubois (Fra)	4:08.6
8. J. Orr (Aus)	4:12.2	U. Klapezynski (GDR)	4:08.8
9. B. Boxem (Hol)	4:13.1	N. Holmen (Fin)	4:08.9
E. Tittel (Ger) Dnf.			

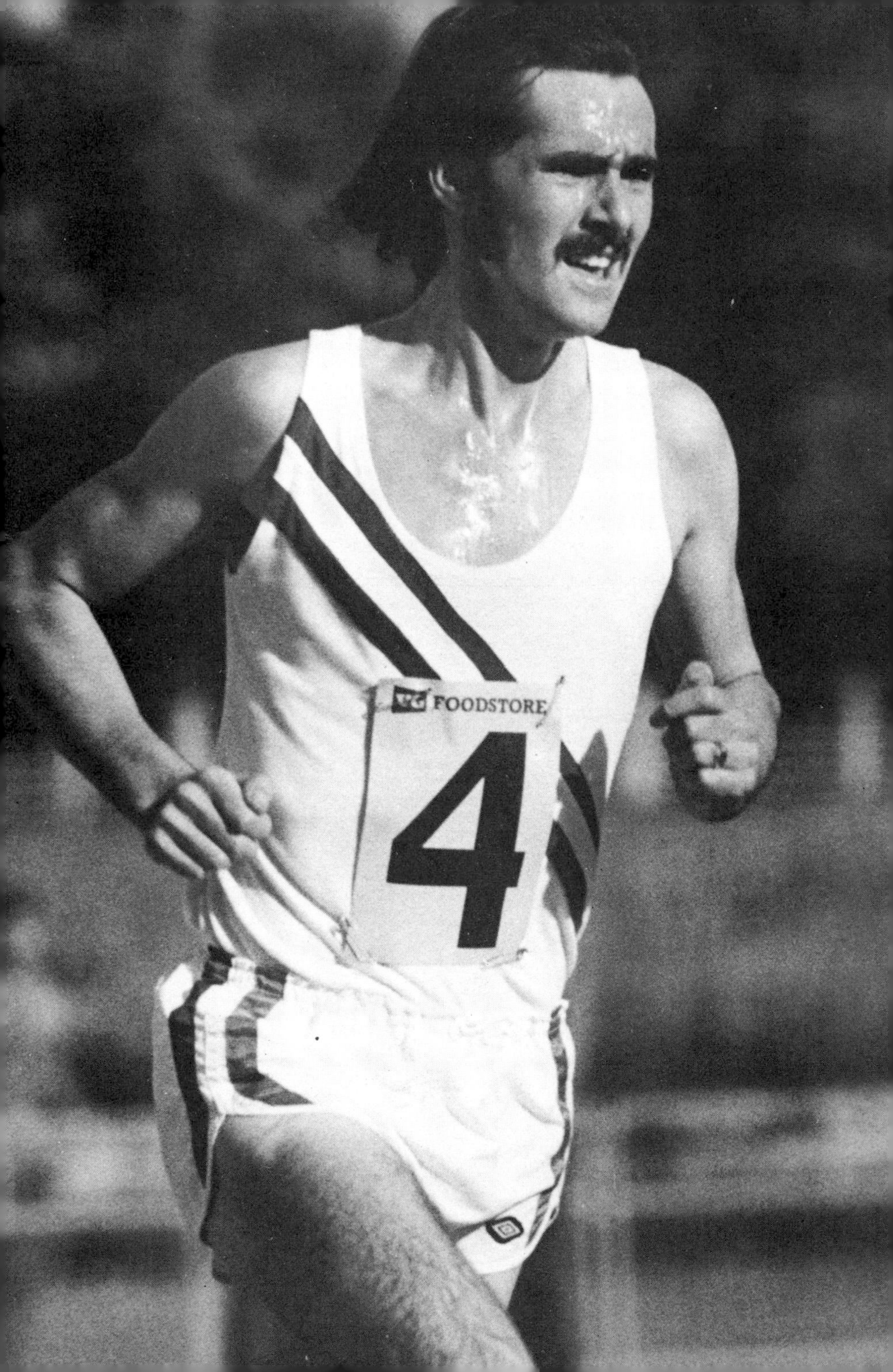
FOODSTORE
4

4. DISTANCE MEN AND CHASERS

The basic simplicity and historic traditions of distance running produces an enormous breadth of talent which makes prediction almost impossible. For many, the sustained excitement of the 5,000 or 10,000 metres makes these the key events and that includes most of the population of Gateshead, home of Britain's Brendan Foster. For 'Big Bren' starts favourite for the 5,000 metres with his devastating tactic of producing three or four 60-second laps in the middle of a race which should be run evenly paced at around 64 seconds each for the 12½ laps. Others who attempt to survive the long burst rarely ride the pressure and Brendan Foster, like David Bedford, often finds the lead a lonely place. But both events are full of talent with the same rugged qualities possessed by Foster. Emiel Puttemans (Belgium), Rod Dixon (NZ) and Ian Stewart (GB) know their task and are just as dedicated to the cause. All could be in contention for the 10,000 metre title, should

Previous page: The greatest talent to emerge from Great Britain over 5,000m is undoubtedly Brendan Foster of Gateshead, seen here beating the Olympic Champion Lasse Viren of Finland, on his way to victory in the European Championships, Rome 1974.

Right: Raelene Boyle of Australia always produces her greatest sprinting when the opposition is at its toughest; it would be a fitting end to her great career if she could top her two Olympic silver medals with a gold in the women's 100 or 200m sprint.

5,000 METRES

Munich 1972		*World Rankings 1975*	
1. L. Viren (Fin)	13:26.4	E. Puttemans (Bel)	13:18.6
2. M. Gammoudi (Tun)	13:27.4	R. Dixon (NZL)	13:21.6
3. I. Stewart (GBR)	13:27.6	K. Boro (Nor)	13:21.8
4. S. Prefontaine (USA)	13:28.4	J. Hermens (Hol)	13:22.4
5. E. Puttemans (Bel)	13:30.8	M. Liquori (USA)	13:23.6
6. H. Norpoth (Ger)	13:32.6	S. Prefontaine (USA)	13:23.8
7. P. Halle (Nor)	13:34.4	A. Garderud (Swe)	13:25.0
8. N. Sviridov (URS)	13:39.4	J. Ngeno (Ken)	13:26.8
9. F. Eisenberg (GDR)	13:40.8	I. Stewart (GBR)	13:27.0
10. J. Alvarez (Esp)	13:41.8	E. Sellik (URS)	13:27.2
11. I. McCafferty (GBR)	13:43.2		
12. D. Bedford (GBR)	13:43.2		
13. J. Vaatainen (Fin)	13:53.8		
M. Haro (Esp) Dns.		Dns. = did not start	

that be their choice, or even for both titles. Lasse Viren of Finland won both in Munich, just as Kolehmainen, Zatopek and Kuts had done in previous Games. It must be a temptation for Foster to seek both titles since his debut at the longer race produced the world's fastest time in 1975 and victory over two other strong contenders — Frank Shorter (USA) and Jos Hermans (Netherlands). Also, it followed a rare defeat for Foster in the 5,000 (by Rod Dixon) in front of his home crowd. Sadly, David Bedford may not have recovered sufficiently from injury to compete; his presence might produce tactical battles in Montreal rather than the expected trials of strength. This situation could play into the hands of fast-finishing Emiel Puttemans or another overnight star from Kenya.

10,000 METRES

Munich 1972		*World Rankings 1975*	
1. L. Viren (Fin)	27:38.4	B. Foster (GBR)	27:45.4
2. E. Puttemans (Bel)	27:39.6	F. Shorter (USA)	27:46.6
3. M. Yifter (Eth)	27:41.0	J. Hermens (Hol)	27:47.6
4. M. Haro (Esp)	27:48.2	D. Black (GBR)	27:53.6
5. F. Shorter (USA)	27:51.4	M. Smet (Bel)	27:53.6
6. D. Bedford (GBR)	28:05.4	K. Boro (Nor)	27:56.2
7. D. Korica (Yug)	28:15.2	J. Brown (GBR)	28:00.6
8. A. Zaddem (Tun)	28:18.2	T. Simmons (GBR)	28:00.8
9. J. Jansky (Tch)	28:23.6	W. Scott (Aus)	28:01.0
10. J-M. Martinez (Mex)	28:44.2	B. Ford (GBR)	28:02.4
11. P. Andreev (URS)	28:46.4	E. Puttemans (Bel)	28:03.6
12. J. Alvarez (Esp)	28:56.4	I. Floroiu (Rom)	28:03.8
13. P. Mose (Ken)	29:03.0	P. Paivarinta (Fin)	28:04.6
14. W. Polleunis (Bel)	29:10.2	J. Ngeno (Ken)	28:04.6
M. Gammoudi (Tun) Dnf.			

The steeplechase suddenly achieved a higher status when Anders Garderud of Sweden shattered the world record twice within a week in June 1975, and Bronislaw Malinowski of Poland also threatened it. Malinowski took the European title and may have the edge as a competitor; in their wake is fast-improving Michael Karst of West Germany, and a host of others.

Left: In the space of one week Anders Garderud of Sweden smashed the world record twice in the 3,000m steeplechase, yet he must still fear the tough Pole Bronislaw Malinowski. Their clash in Montreal should produce a 'classic'.

Below: Bronislaw Malinowski, European champion of the 3,000m steeplechase in Rome, 1974.

3,000 METRES STEEPLECHASE

Munich 1972		*World Rankings 1975*	
1. K. Keino (Ken)	8:23.6	A. Garderud (Swe)	8:09.8
2. B. Jipcho (Ken)	8:24.6	B. Malinowski (Pol)	8:12.6
3. T. Kantanen (Fin)	8:24.8	M. Karst (Ger)	8:16.2
4. B. Malinowski (Pol)	8:28.0	G. Cefan (Rom)	8:17.6
5. D. Moravcik (Tch)	8:29.2	F. Baumgartl (GDR)	8:17.6
6. A. Biwott (Ken)	8:33.6	T. Kantanen (Fin)	8:18.0
7. R. Bitte (URS)	8:34.6	Y. Mohamed (Eth)	8:19.6
8. P. Paivarinta (Fin)	8:37.2	J. Straub (GDR)	8:19.8
9. T. Koyama (Jpn)	8:37.8	F. Fava (Ita)	8:20.4
10. M. Ala-Leppilampi (Fin)	8:41.0	A. Campos (Esp)	8:21.6
11. J.-P. Villain (Fra)	8:46.8		
12. M. Jelev (Bul)	9:02.6		

5. MARATHONERS

In the marathon a classic confrontation is expected between two runners. Frank Shorter's emphatic victory in Munich was the first from the US since 1908 and he has a great following. Ian Thompson (GB) of Luton United Harriers ran his first marathon in 1973; he won that, as well as his four other marathon attempts, which included the Commonwealth Games and the European Championships! Both Shorter and Thompson took an easy season in 1975, so their long-awaited duel in Montreal will provide great excitement. However, the experience of Lismont (Belgium), Ron Hill (GB), as well as Rodgers and Hoag of the US and Derek Clayton of Australia means a very tough pack will give chase. No event is more vulnerable to injury or more likely to produce drama than this one, which covers 42.195 metres (26 miles, 385 yards).

MARATHON

Munich 1972		World Rankings 1975	
1. F. Shorter (USA)	2:12:19.8	W. Rodgers (USA)	2:09.55
2. K. Lismont (Bel)	2:14:31.8	S. Hoag (USA)	2:11.54
3. M. Wolde (Eth)	2:15:08.4	T. Fleming (USA)	2:12:05
4. K. Moore (USA)	2:15:39.8	H. Rodrigues (Col)	2:12:08
5. K. Kimihara (Jpn)	2:16:27.0	R. Hill (GBR)	2:12:34
6. R. Hill (GBR)	2:16:30.6	A. Usami (Jpn)	2:12:40
7. D. MacGregor (GBR)	2:16:34.4		
8. J. Foster (NZL)	2:16:56.2		
9. J. Bacheler (USA)	2:17:38.2		
10. L. Bedane (Eth)	2:18:36.8		
11. S. Nikkari (Fin)	2:18:49.4		
12. A. Usami (Jpn)	2:18:58.0		

Right: The Soviet Union's Valeriy Borzov (932) has been described as a scientifically-created sprinter, yet his form here is near perfect — relaxed arms, shoulders, neck and face, with all the explosion coming from his powerful legs.

Frank Shorter (above) was the first US runner to win the marathon since 1908, and since 1972 he has proved invincible; yet Ian Thompson of Great Britain (left) has equally impeccable credentials — he has run only five marathons, including the 1974 Commonwealth Games and 1974 European Championships, and has won all five!

6. JUMPERS

High Jump The history of the high jump is a tribute to man's athletic ingenuity. He started with a clumsy scissors-style jump and progressed through the eastern cut-off, western roll and straddle. Just when the world's coaches were convinced that jumpers had reached the ultimate in bio-mechanical efficiency along came Dick Fosbury of the US with the Fosbury 'flop' and Debbie Brill of Canada with the Brill 'bend' to shatter their illusions. Now it is as much a battle between styles as places.

Both men's and women's events in Montreal have firm favourites in Dwight Stones of the US, a 'flopper', and Rosemarie Witschas Ackermann of East Germany, a straddle jumper. Dwight Stones can claim eight of the best 14 jumps in history and holds both the indoor

HIGH JUMP (Men)

Munich 1972				*World Rankings 1975*		
1.	Y. Tarmak (URS)	2.23	7'3¾	D. Stones (USA)	2.28	7'5¾
2.	S. Junge (GDR)	2.21	7'3	T. Woods (USA)	2.27	7'5¼
3.	D. Stones (USA)	2.21	7'3	P. Poaniewa (Fra)	2.26	7'5
4.	H. Magerl (Ger)	2.18	7'1¾	P. Matzdorf (USA)	2.24	7'4¼
5.	A. Szepesi (Hun)	2.18	7'1¾	R. Beilschmidt (GDR)	2.24	7'4¼
6.	I. Major (Hun)	2.15	7'0½	R. Livers (USA)	2.24	7'4¼
6.	J. Beers (Can)	2.15	7'0½	A. Grigoryev (URS)	2.24	7'4¼
8.	R. Akhmetov (URS)	2.15	7'0½	J. Maly (Tch)	2.24i	7'4¼
9.	J. Hawkins (Can)	2.15	7'0½	W. Jankunis (USA)	2.23	7'4
10.	E. Dal Forno (Ita)	2.15	7'0½	R. Kotinek (USA)	2.23	7'4
11.	J. Dahlgren (Swe)	2.15	7'0½	J. Wszola (Pol)	2.23	7'4
12.	V. Papadimitriou (Gre)	2.15	7'0½	K. Guinn (USA)	2.23	7'4
12.	K. Shapka (URS)	2.15	7'0½	B. Brokken (Bel)	2.23	7'4
14.	B. Gauthier (Fra)	2.15	7'0½	G. Joy (Can)	2.23i	7'4
				R. Alman (Swe)	2.23i	7'4

i = indoor

HIGH JUMP (Women)

Munich 1972				*World Rankings 1975*		
1.	U. Meyfarth (Ger)	1.92	6'3½	R. Witchas Ackermann (GDR)	1.94	6'4¼
2.	Y. Balgoeva (Bul)	1.88	6'2	U. Meyfarth (Ger)	1.92	6'3½
3.	I. Gusenbauer (Aut)	1.88	6'2	J. Huntley (USA)	1.90	6'2¾
4.	B. Inkpen (GBR)	1.85	6'0¾	N. Oskolok (URS)	1.89	6'2¼
5.	R. Schmidt (GDR)	1.85	6'0¾	D. Brill (Can)	1.89	6'2¼
6.	S. Simeoni (Ita)	1.85	6'0¾	S. Simeoni (Ita)	1.89	6'2¼
7.	R. Witschas (GDR)	1.85	6'0¾	Diane Jones (Can)	1.88	6'2
8.	D. Brill (Can)	1.82	5'11¾	Louise Walker (Can)	1.88	6'2
9.	A. Bruce (Jam)	1.82	5'11¾	M. Van Doorn (Hol)	1.88	6'2
10.	E. Mundinger (Ger)	1.82	5'11¾	A. Fedorchuk (URS)	1.88	6'2
11.	A. Reid (Jam)	1.82	5'11¾			
12.	R. Gildemeister (GDR)	1.82	5'11¾			

Below: One of the few men to start clear favourite in Montreal is high jumper Dwight Stones of the United States; he is current world record holder at 2.30m.

Right: Filbert Bayi (613) of Tanzania, taking the victory at 1,500m over John Walker (483) of New Zealand in an epic race at the Commonwealth Games in Christchurch, 1974.

Below: Rosemarie Witschas Ackermann of
East Germany, reigning world record holder
and European champion in the high jump,
looks a sure winner in Montreal, but Ulrike
Meyfarth of West Germany could again come
from behind to win the gold, as she did in
Munich.

and outdoor world records. Rosemarie Witschas Ackermann, reigning European Champion, is just as consistent and also holds both indoor and outdoor world records. She will be challenged by Olympic champion Ulrike Meyfarth of West Germany; Stone's nearest rivals appear to be Tom Woods of the US and Paul Paoniwa of France. Canada also has great strength in high jumping with Greg Joy, whose record is 7ft 4in, and Debbie Brill, Diane Jones and Louise Walker, all with records over 6ft 2in.

Long jump At Mexico City in 1968, Bob Beamon of the US made a jump which must rank as one of the athletic feats of the century. It was an incredible 8.90 metres (29ft 2½in) — a record which survived Munich and could survive the rest of this century! In Munich an anti-climactic men's long jump produced the youngest winner of any men's event in Randy Williams of the US, while in the women's event Heide Rosendahl of West Germany came to the fore. Her world record of 6.84 metres (22ft 5¼in) was set in 1970 and could survive in Montreal.

Although the long jump is an event demanding great sprinting speed and explosive power for vertical lift, it also demands a controlled take-off from as near to the front edge of the eight-inch board as possible. The discipline required for this take-off can be an inhibiting factor. In 1975 there were three men jumping at well over 27 feet — Ehizuelen of Nigeria, Cybulski of Poland, and the best talent around, Nenad Stekic of Yugoslavia who broke the European record with a jump of 27ft 8¾in, and who should win in Montreal.

In the women's event, only Lidiya Alfyeva of the USSR and Isobella Lusti of Switzerland bettered 22 feet during 1975, and they will be strong contenders for the gold medal in Montreal. However, the

LONG JUMP (Men)

Munich 1972			*World Rankings 1975*		
1. R. Williams (USA)	8.24	27'0½	N. Stekic (Yug)	8.45	27'8¾
2. H. Baumgartner (Ger)	8.18	26'10	A. Robinson (USA)	(8.28) 8.35w	27'4¾
3. A. Robinson (USA)	8.03	26'4¾	C. Ehizuelan (Nig)	(8.26i) 8.33w	27'4
3. J. Owusu (Gha)	8.01	26'3½	G. Cybulski (Pol)	8.27	27'1¼
5. P. Carrington (USA)	7.99	26'2¾	D. Seay (USA)	(8.13) 8.21w	26'11¼
6. M. Klauss (GDR)	7.96	26'1½	J. Oliveira (Bra)	8.20	26'11
7. A. Lerwill (GBR)	7.91	25'11½	T. Hamilton (USA)	(8.11i) 8.18w	26'10
8. L. Barkovski (URS)	7.75	25'5¼	V. Podluzhnyi (URS)	8.12w	26'7¾
9. V. Podluzhnyi (URS)	7.72	25'4	T. Haynes (USA)	8.09w	26'8½
10. J. Rousseau (Fra)	7.65	25'1¼	L. C. de Souza (Bra)	8.08	26'6¼
11. A. Vaeaenaenen (Fin)	7.62	25'0			
12. G. Cybulski (Pol)	7.58	24'10½			

w = wind-assisted
i = indoor

LONG JUMP (Women)

Munich 1972			*World Rankings 1975*		
1. H. Rosendahl (Ger)	6.78	22'3	I. Lusti (Sui)	(6.65) 6.82w	22'4½
2. D. Yorgova (Bul)	6.77	22'2½	L. Alfeyeva (URS)	6.76	22'2¼
3. E. Suranova (Tch)	6.67	21'10¾	I. Szabo (Hun)	6.66	21'10¼
4. M. Garbey (Cub)	6.52	21'4¾	A. Alexander (Cub)	6.63	21'9
5. H. Schueller (Ger)	6.51	21'4¼	A. Voigt (GDR)	6.61	21'8¼
6. M. Antenen (Sui)	6.49	21'3½	I. Bruzsenyak (Hun)	6.61w	21'8¼
7. V. Viscopoleanu (Rom)	6.48	21'3¼	K. McMillan (USA)	6.58	21'7½
8. M. Olfert (GDR)	6.46	21'2½	M. Garbey (Cub)	6.57	21'6¾
9. S. Sherwood (GBR)	6.41	21'0½	M. Watson (USA)	6.57	21'6¾
10. I. Bruzsenyak (Hun)	6.39	20'11¾	C. Striezel (Ger)	6.56	21'6¼
11. W. White (USA)	6.27	20'7	M. Dlugosieska (Pol)	6.54	21'5½
12. J. Nygrynova (Tch)	6.24	20'5¾	S. G. Pereira (Bra)	6.50	21'3½

w = wind assisted

competition is close and both events will be open for grabs to the best man and woman on the day.

Triple jump The powerful Victor Saneyev of the USSR has long dominated the triple jump. He has rarely been beaten and he was the only man in Munich to defend his Olympic title successfully. Just as it was becoming a matter of deciding who would come second to Saneyev at Montreal, the brilliant Brazilian bombshell Joao Oliveira did a 'Beamon' in Mexico City's rarified atmosphere at the 1975 Pan American Games with a leap of 17.89 metres (58ft 8½in) shattering Saneyev's world record by 18 inches! There is now great debate as to

Below left: Anna Alexander of Cuba was the surprise winner of the long jump in the Pan Am Games in October 1975. Below right: The only male athlete successfully to defend his Olympic title in Munich was the supreme technician at the triple jump, Viktor Saneyev of the Soviet Union, but even he must have been astonished to see his world record beaten by 18 inches by Brazil's Joao Oliveira in the Pan Am Games in 1975.

Right: No athlete in Montreal will have a greater following in the 5,000m than Brendan Foster of Great Britain, but he may face an embarrassment of choice, since during 1975 he produced the world's fastest time at 10,000m.

what extent altitude affected Oliveira's jump and whether he can repeat it at Montreal. I have no doubt that Saneyev will respond to the challenge but Oliveira is the most fluent triple jumper I have ever seen — yet another great duel appears in prospect.

TRIPLE JUMP

Munich 1972			World Rankings 1975		
1. V. Saneyev (URS)	17.35	56'11¼	J. Oliveira (Bra)	17.89	58'8½
2. J. Drehmel (GDR) *	17.31	56'9½	V. Saneyev (URS)	17.33	56'10¼
3. N. Prudencio (Bra)	17.05	55'11¼	T. Haynes (USA)	17.20	56'5¼
4. C. Corbu (Rom)	16.85	55'3½	M. Joachimowski (Pol)		
5. J. Craft (USA)	16.83	55'2¼	(16.90i)	17.04w	55'11
6. M. Dia (Sen)	16.83	55'2¾	J. Drehmel (GDR)	16.98	55'8½
7. N. Joachimowski (Pol)	16.69	54'9¼	A. Rahman (USA)	16.98	55'8½
8. K. Floegstad (Nor)	16.44	53'11¼	A. Sontag (Pol)	16.96	55'7¾
9. M. Bariban (URS)	16.30	53'5¼	N. Prudencia (Bra)	16.93	55'6¼
10. B. Lamitie (Fra)	16.27	53'4½	E. Biskupski (Pol)	16.92	55'6¼
11. S. Igun (Nig)	16.03	52'7¼	N. Sinichkin (URS)	16.88	55'4¾
12. T. Inoue (Jpn)	15.88	52'1¼	P. Kuukasjarvi (Fin)	16.87	55'4¼
			A. Grimes (USA)	16.86	55'3¾
			C. Corbu (Rom)	16.82	55'2¼

w = wind-assisted

7. VAULTERS

Below: US pole vaulter Dave Roberts, current world record holder at 5.65m, starts favourite in Montreal, but Europe provides a tough challenger in Wladislaw Kozakiewicz of Poland.

When US vaulters Bob Seagren and Steve Smith turned professional, the pole vault appeared to have lost a lot of its glamour but the US produced four 18-foot vaulters in one season as replacements! Dan Ripley had an amazing rise from 16ft 3in to 17ft 8in in one competition, and only weeks later became the world's eighth 18-foot vaulter. No sooner had the US outdoor season begun when along came big blond left-hander David Roberts to break Seagren's world record with a jump of 5.65 metres (18ft 6½in). Wladislaw Kozakiewicz of Poland is only 5cm lower with a European record of 5.60 metres, so it could be another battle between the US and eastern Europe, though Australia's Don Baird also has an outside chance of a medal.

POLE VAULT

Munich 1972				World Rankings 1975		
1. W. Nordwig (GDR)	5.50	18'0½		D. Roberts (USA)	5.65	18'6½
2. R. Seagren (USA)	5.40	17'8½		W. Kozakiewicz (Pol)	5.60	18'4½
3. J. Johnson (USA)	5.35	17'6½		V. Dias (USA)	5.51	18'1
4. R. Kuretzky (Ger)	5.30	17'4½		E. Bell (USA)	5.51	18'1
5. B. Simpson (Can)	5.20	17'0¾		D. Ripley (USA)	5.51	18'1
6. V. Ohl (Ger)	5.20	17'0¾		W. Buciarski (Pol)	5.50	18'0½
7. H. Lagerqvist (Swe)	5.20	17'0¾		L. Jessee (USA)	5.49	18'0
8. F. Tracanelli (Fra)	5.10	16'8¾		R. Rogers (USA)	5.48	17'11¾
9. I. Jernberg (Swe)	5.10	16'8¾		V. Trofimenka (URS)	5.46	17'11
10. W. Buciarski (Pol)	5.00	16'4¾		C. Carrigan (USA)	5.45	17'10½
11. C. Papanikolaou (Gre)	5.00	16'4¾		V. Kishkun (URS)	5.45	17'10½
				M. Tully (USA)	5.43	17'9¾
				V. Boiko (URS)	5.45i	17'9¾

i = indoor

8. THROWERS

Shot The shot produces the biggest and strongest athletes in the world, for size and strength, as well as speed and technique, are absolute prerequisites. Sadly, the event has fallen into disrepute because of its identity with the growing use of anabolic steroid drugs. It can only be hoped that adequate and fair testing procedures will be adopted to protect both the sport and the athletes in Montreal.

At Munich no event was closer than the men's shot; Wladislaw Komar of Poland beat George Woods of the US by a mere centimetre; it was only the third defeat for the US in this event since 1896. Woods will doubtless be back with a vengeance, along with current world record holder Al Feuerbach of the US, who was injured for most of the 1975 season. Sweden's Hoglund made one put of almost 70ft which topped the 1975 rankings, but in competition he was well beaten during the rest of the season. Europe will stage a strong

SHOT (Men)

Munich 1972			*World Rankings 1975*		
1. W. Komar (Pol)	21.18	69'6	H. Hoglund (Swe)	21.33	69'11¾
2. G. Woods (USA)	21.17	69'5½	A. Feuerbach (USA)	21.25	69'8¾
3. H. Briesenick (GDR)	21.14	69'4¼	H-J. Rothenburg (GDR)	20.98	68'10
4. H-P. Gies (GDR)	21.14	69'4¼	U. Beyer (GDR)	20.97	68'9¾
5. A. Feuerbach (USA)	21.01	68'11¼	H. Briesenick (GDR)	20.96	68'9¼
6. B. Oldfield (USA)	20.91	68'7¼	H-P. Gies (GDR)	20.92	68'7¾
7. H. Birlenbach (Ger)	20.37	66'10	G. Capes (GBR)	20.80	68'3
8. V. Varju (Hun)	20.10	65'11½	T. Albritton (USA)	20.75	68'1
9. J. Vlk (Tch)	20.09	65'11	J. Stuart (USA)	20.73i	68'0¾
10. J. Brabec (Tch)	19.86	65'2	J. Brabec (Tch)	20.45	67'1¼
11. H. Rothenburg (GDR)	19.74	64'9¼	W. Komar (Pol)	20.44	67'1
12. Y. Brouzet (Fra)	19.61	64'4	G. Woods (USA)	20.43	67'0½

i = indoor

SHOT (Women)

Munich 1972			*World Rankings 1975*		
1. N. Chizhova (URS)	21.03	69'0	M. Adam (GDR)	21.60	70'10½
2. M. Gummel (GDR)	20.22	66'4¼	H. Fibingerova (Tch)	21.43	70'3¾
3. I. Khristova (Bul)	19.35	63'6	I. Khristova (Bul)	21.09	69'2½
4. E. Dolzhenko (URS)	19.24	63'1½	E. Krachevskaya (URS)	21.02	68'11¾
5. M. Adam (GDR)	18.94	62'1¾	I. Schoknecht (GDR)	20.12	66'0¼
6. M. Lange (GDR)	18.85	61'10¼	F. Melnik (URS)	19.88	65'2¾
7. H. Fibingerova (Tch)	18.81	61'8½	B. Loewe (GDR)	19.73	64'8¾
8. E. Stoyanova (Bul)	18.34	60'2	M. Droese (GDR)	19.71	64'8
9. A. Ivanova (URS)	18.28	59'11¾	Y. Stoyanova (Bul)	19.46	63'10¼
10. L. Chewinska (Pol)	18.24	59'10¼	M. Loghin (Rom)	19.15	62'10
11. J. Bognar (Hun)	18.23	59'9¼			
12. R. Vassekova (Bul)	17.86	58'7¼			
13. V. Cioltan (Rom)	16.62	54'6½			

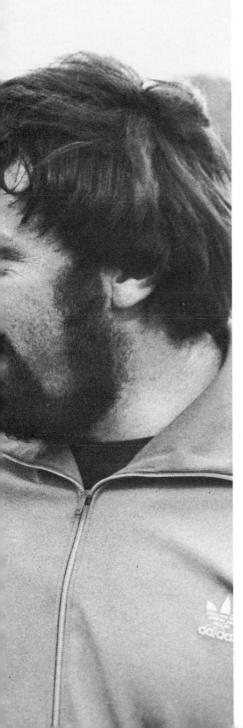

Left: The Iowa farm boy Al Feuerbach (left), reigning world record holder in the shot, and one of his closest rivals, Cambridge policeman Geoffrey Capes, who is Britain's best chance of a field event medal. Below: Marianne Adam of East Germany (top) has finally broken the Soviet Union's stranglehold in the women's shot and starts favourite in Montreal, as does Faina Melnik (bottom) in the discus where Soviet supremacy will remain undisputed.

challenge with Briesenick, Rothenburg and Beyer from East Germany, and with Geoffrey Capes of Great Britain, a Cambridge policeman who is Britain's best chance of a field event medal.

In the women's event, the Russian stranglehold appears to have been broken by Helena Fibingerova of Czechoslovakia and Marianne Adam of East Germany, who is the present world record holder with a throw of 21.60 metres (70ft 10½in).

Discus Success in the discus is an intricate affair, dependent upon the angle and trajectory of flight, which stems from critical balance and timing. Again, the US has lost the title only three times and at one stage Al Oerter appeared to have made it his personal property. In Munich, 35-year-old Ludvik Danek of Czechoslovakia finally won the title at his third attempt; in 1975 he threw 10 feet further than his winning throw at Munich, so he is still very much in contention. The

DISCUS (Men)

Munich 1972			*World Rankings 1975*		
1. L. Danek (Tch)	64.40	211'3	J. Powell (USA)	69.10	226'8
2. J. Silvester (USA)	63.50	208'4	J. VanReenen (SA)	68.48	224'8
3. R. Bruch (Swe)	63.40	208'0	L. Danek (Tch)	67.14	220'3
4. J. Powell (USA)	62.82	206'1	R. Bruch (Swe)	66.88	219'5
5. G. Fejer (Hun)	62.62	205'5	P. Kahma (Fin)	66.84	219'3
6. D. Thorith (GDR)	62.42	204'9	W. Schmidt (GDR)	66.80	219'2
7. F. Tegla (Hun)	60.60	198'10	M. Wilkins (USA)	66.78	219'1
8. T. Vollmer (USA)	60.24	197'8	M. Tuokko (Fin)	66.40	217'10
9. P. Kahma (Fin)	59.66	195'9	S. Pachale (GDR)	66.04	216'8
10. S. Simeon (Ita)	59.34	194'8	B. Dolegiewicz (Can)	65.32	214'4
11. J. Rinne (Fin)	59.22	194'3	V. Velev (Bul)	65.16	213'9
12. J. Muranyi (Hun)	57.92	190'0			

DISCUS (Women)

Munich 1972			*World Rankings 1975*		
1. F. Melnik (URS)	66.62	218'7	F. Melnik (URS)	70.20	230'4
2. A. Menis (Rom)	65.06	213'5	A. Menis (Rom)	67.88	222'8
3. V. Stoeva (Bul)	64.34	211'1	S. Engel (GDR)	67.34	220'11
4. T. Danilova (URS)	62.86	206'3	M. Vergova (Bul)	66.98	219'9
5. L. Westermann (Ger)	62.18	204'0	G. Hinzmann (GDR)	66.98	219'9
6. G. Hinzmann (GDR)	61.72	202'6	C. Romero (Cub)	66.80	219'2
7. C. Ionescu (Rom)	60.42	198'3	O. Andrianova (URS)	63.90	209'8
8. L. Muraviova (URS)	59.00	193'7	C. Ionesco (Can)	63.68	208'11
9. L. Manoliu (Rom)	58.50	191'11	E. Schlaak (GDR)	63.44	208'2
10. S. Bochkova (Bul)	56.72	186'1	H. Vyhnalova (Tch)	63.26	207'6
11. B. Berendonk (Ger)	56.58	185'7	A. Braun (GDR)	63.22	207'5
12. R. Payne (GBR)	56.50	185'4			

world record changed hands twice in 1975 and it rests now with the smoothest technician around — John Powell of the US, a San José policeman who at 6ft 2in and 240lb is relatively small! Powell starts favourite, followed by European champion Pentti Kahma of Finland and Wolfgang Schmidt of East Germany. (South African Van Reenan will not be competing.) The women's event looks to be a very much one-sided affair. Faina Melnik of the USSR has been breaking the world record with almost monotonous regularity and looks unbeatable.

Javelin The surprise defeat of Janis Lusis of the USSR in Munich by Klaus Wolfermann of West Germany ended an era. Wolfermann further proved his worth by also taking the world record, but he did not have a good season in 1975. Nikolay Grebnyev of the USSR at 6ft 4in and 224lb looks very impressive, while Miklos Nemeth of Hungary tops the rankings. Finland have a marvellous chance to add to their

JAVELIN (Men)

Munich 1972			World Rankings 1975		
1. K. Wolfermann (Ger)	90.48	296'10	M. Nemeth (Hun)	91.38	299'10
2. J. Lusis (URS)	90.46	296'9	H. Siitonen (Fin)	90.22	296'0
3. W. Schmidt (USA)	84.42	276'11	F. Paragi (Hun)	89.92	295'0
4. H. Siitonen (Fin)	84.32	276'7	V. Yershov (URS)	89.00	292'0
5. B. Grimnes (Nor)	83.08	272'7	S. Hovinen (Fin)	88.48	290'3
6. J. Kinnunen (Fin)	82.08	269'3	A. Yerebtov (URS)	86.92	285'2
7. M. Nemeth (Hun)	81.98	268'11	A. Makarov (URS)	86.70	284'5
8. F. Luke (USA)	80.06	262'8	S. Boros (Hun)	86.60	284'1
9. M. Stolle (GDR)	79.32	260'3	N. Grebnyev (URS)	86.56	284'0
10. M. Sonsky (USA)	77.94	255'8	A. Aho (Fin)	85.74	281'3
11. L. Tuita (Fra)	76.34	250'5			
12. J. Csik (Hun)	76.14	249'9			

JAVELIN (Women)

Munich 1972			World Rankings 1975		
1. R. Fuchs (GDR)	63.88	209'7	R. Fuchs (GDR)	66.46	218'0
2. J. Todten (GDR)	62.54	205'2	K. Schmidt (USA)	63.88	209'7
3. K. Schmidt (USA)	59.94	196'8	T. Shigalova (URS)	63.22	207'5
4. L. Mollova (Bul)	59.36	194'9	S. Babich (URS)	63.02	206'9
5. N. Urbancic (Yug)	59.06	193'9	L. Mollova (Bul)	62.32	204'5
6. E. Janko (Aut)	58.56	192'1	J. Todten (GDR)	62.24	204'2
7. E. Gryziecka (Pol)	57.00	187'0	M. Becker (Ger)	61.18	200'9
8. S. Koroliova (URS)	56.36	184'11	E. Gryziecka (Pol)	61.14	200'7
9. A. Gerhards (Ger)	55.84	183'2	D. Kuryan (URS)	61.12	200'6
10. M. Kucserka (Hun)	54.40	178'6	I. Pecec (Rom)	60.98	200'1
11. M. Paulanyi (Hun)	52.36	171'9			

Below: Leading a trio of impressive Soviet hammer throwers is likely to be Alexei Spiridinov, the reigning European champion.

Right: The man who did another 'Beamon' in Mexico City, 1975, Joao Oliveira of Brazil, whose new world record for the triple jump stands at an incredible 17.89m (58ft 8¼in).

five past successes in the event they cherish most with any one of Hannu Siitonen, Seppo Hovinen or Aimo Aho.

In the women's event Ruth Fuchs of East Germany, like Faina Melnik in the discus, has all the credentials to retain her title. She will again be chased by Kathy Schmidt of the US and Jacqueline Todten of East Germany.

Hammer The hammer throw is a sophisticated event which has its origins in early British rural sports. In an amazing 1975 season Karl-Heinz Riehm of West Germany broke the existing world record six times in six throws, and then lost it to Walter Schmidt, his fellow countryman, less than two weeks later! Yet it would be wrong to assume that the event will be an all-German affair in Montreal, for the ranking lists are full of world class throwers from the USSR, any one of whom could snatch the title. I predict a battle between Riehm and the European champion, Spiridinov of the USSR.

Left: Karl-Heinz Riehm (West Germany) set a unique record in the history of track and field during 1975 when he shattered the world record for the hammer six times in six throws.

HAMMER

Munich 1972				World Rankings 1975		
1.	A. Bondarchuk (URS)	75.50	247'8	W. Schmidt (Ger)	79.30	260'2
2.	J. Sachse (GDR)	74.96	245'11	K-H. Riehm (Ger)	78.50	257'6
3.	V. Khmelevski (URS)	74.04	242'11	D. Pkhakadze (URS)	77.64	254'9
4.	U. Beyer (Ger)	71.52	234'8	V. Dmitrenko (URS)	77.58	254'6
5.	G. Zsivotzky (Hun)	71.38	234'2	A. Spiridinov (URS)	76.84	252'1
6.	S. Eckschmiedt (Hun)	71.20	233'7	V. Valentyuk (URS)	76.60	251'4
7.	E. Klein (Ger)	71.14	233'5	J. Sachse (GDR)	76.40	250'8
8.	S. Murofushi (Jpn)	70.88	232'6	M. Huning (Ger)	75.78	248'7
9.*	M. Vecchiato (Ita)	70.58	231'7	V. Khmelevskiy (URS)	74.98	246'0
10.	K-H. Riehm (Ger)	70.12	230'1	Y. Sedykh (URS)	74.30	243'9
11.	I. Encsi (Hun)	70.06	229'10	A. Bondarchuk (URS)	73.80	242'1
12.	T. Gage (USA)	69.50	228'0			

9. WALKERS

The walking fraternity are still smarting at the loss of the 50 kilometre walk from the Olympic calendar, leaving them only the 20 kilometre event. Since Britain won the 50 kilometre walk three times out of eight and New Zealand won it once, it is a sad loss to the Commonwealth. In the 20 kilometre walk Mexico has a great chance of their first track and field gold medal with Daniel Bautista, Domingo Colin or Angel Flores who were ranked first, second and third in 1975. However, Bernd Kannenberg, winner of the 50 kilometre walk in Munich, is now the world record holder at 20 kilometres and Peter Frenkel of East Germany should be fit to defend his Olympic title.

10. ALL-ROUNDERS

Britain's sole gold medallist in Munich was Mary Peters, who won the women's all round championship — the pentathlon (100 metre hurdles, shot, high jump, long jump, 200 metre sprint). Now Canada have high hopes with Diane Jones, but Burglinde Pollak of East Germany is the world record holder with 4932 points, and looks very strong.

In the men's all round championship, the decathlon, Nikolai Avilov of the USSR took the title and world record in Munich but he has

PENTATHLON

Munich 1972			World Rankings 1975	
1. M. Peters (GBR)	4801		B. Pollak (GDR)	4787
2. H. Rosendahl (Ger)	4791		N. Tkachenko (URS)	4698
3. B. Pollak (GDR)	4768		J. Frederick (USA)	4676
4. C. Bodner (GDR)	4671		D. Jones (Can)	4673
5. V. Tikhomirova (URS)	4597		S. Thon (GDR)	4636
6. N. Anghelova (Bul)	4496		C. Laser (GDR)	4635
7 K. Mack (Ger)	4449		L. Prokop (Aus)	4579
8. I. Bruzsenyak (Hun)	4419		A. Seeger (GDR)	4573
9. N. Tkachenko (URS)	4370		B. Muller (GDR)	4561
10. D. Jones (Can)	4349		L. Popovskaya (URS)	4553
11. D. Focic (Yug)	4332		M. Eppinger (Ger)	4551
12. M. Eppinger (Ger)	4313			

since lost the world record to Bruce Jenner of the US and been beaten by US second-runner Fred Dixon. Many track and field enthusiasts regard this as the greatest medal; it is fought over two days and ten events (100 metres, long jump, shot, high jump, 400 metres, 110 metres hurdles, discus, pole vault, javelin and 1,500 metres). The climax of the event will likely find the US and the USSR in hot contention.

DECATHLON

Munich 1972			World Rankings 1975	
1. N. Avilov (URS)	8454		B. Jenner (USA)	8524
2. L. Litvinenko (URS)	8035		F. Dixon (USA)	8277
3. R. Katus (Pol)	7984		N. Avilov (URS)	8229
4. J. Bennett (USA)	7974		R. Skowronek (Pol)	8185
5. S. Schreyer (GDR)	7950		L. Litvinenko (URS)	8152
6. F. Herbrand (Bel)	7947			
7. S. Jensen (Den)	7947			
8. T. Janczenko (Pol)	7861			
9. J. Zeilbauer (Aut)	7741			
10. B. Jenner (USA)	7722			
11. R. Ghesquiere (Bel)	7677			
12. Y. Leroy (Fra)	7675			

Right: Scotland's David Wilkie captured a
silver medal in the Munich Olympics and two
world titles in Cali in July 1975; he carries
British Olympic hopes for gold medals in the
100 and 200m breaststroke, as well as being a
key figure in Britain's 4 x 100m medley relay
team. In Montreal he will be competing
against his perennial rival, John Hencken of
the US.

Olympic Track and Field Records and Best Performances

MEN

Event	Record	Athlete	Location	Year
100m	9.9	Jim Hines (USA)	Mexico City	1968
200m	19.8	T. Smith (USA)	Mexico City	1968
400m	43.8	L. Evans (USA)	Mexico City	1968
800m	1:44.3	R. Doubell (Aus)	Mexico City	1968
1,500m	3:34.9	K. Keino (Ken)	Mexico City	1968
5,000m	13:26.4	L. Viren (Fin)	Munich	1972
10,000m	27:38.4	L. Viren (Fin)	Munich	1972
Marathon	2:12:11.2	A. Bikila (Eth)	Tokyo	1964
Steeplechase	8:23.6	K. Keino (Ken)	Munich	1972
110m hurdles	13.24	R. Milburn (USA)	Munich	1972
400m hurdles	47.82	J. Akii-Bua (Uga)	Munich	1972
4 x 100m relay	38.19	USA	Munich	1972
4 x 400m relay	2:56.1	USA	Mexico City	1968
High Jump	2m 24	R. Fosbury (USA)	Mexico City	1968
Long Jump	8m 90	R. Beamon (USA)	Mexico City	1968
Triple Jump	17m 39	V. Saneyev (URS)	Mexico City	1968
Pole Vault	5m 50	W. Nordwig (GDR)	Munich	1972
Shot	21m 18	W. Komar (Pol)	Munich	1972
Discus	64m 78	A. Oerter (USA)	Mexico City	1968
Hammer	75m 50	A. Bondarchuk (URS)	Munich	1972
Javelin	90m 48	K. Wolfermann (Ger)	Munich	1972
Decathlon	8454pts	N. Avilov (URS)	Munich	1972
20km walk	1:26:42.4	P. Frenkel (GDR)	Munich	1972
50km walk	3:56:11.6	B. Kannenberg (Ger)	Munich	1972

WOMEN

Event	Record	Athlete	Location	Year
100m	11.0	W. Tyus (USA)	Mexico City	1968
200m	22.4	R. Stecher (GDR)	Munich	1972
400m	51.08	M. Zehrt (GDR)	Munich	1972
800m	1:58.6	H. Falck (Ger)	Munich	1972
1,500m	4:01.4	L. Bragina (URS)	Munich	1972
100m hurdles	12.59	A. Erhardt (GDR)	Munich	1972
4 x 100m relay	42.8	USA and	Mexico City	1968
		Ger	Munich	1972
4 x 400m relay	3:23.0	GDR	Munich	1972
High Jump	1m 92	U. Meyfarth (Ger)	Munich	1972
Long Jump	6m 82	V. Viscopoleanu (Rom)	Mexico City	1968
Shot	21m 03	N. Chizhova (URS)	Munich	1972
Discus	66m 62	F. Melnik (URS)	Munich	1972
Javelin	63m 88	R. Fuchs (GDR)	Munich	1972
Pentathlon	4801 pts	M. Peters (GBR)	Munich	1972

TRACK AND FIELD RECORDS: As of November 1st 1975

(W) World; (E) European; (C) Commonwealth; (UK) United Kingdom.

Men

100 METRES

(W) 9.9
Jim Hines (USA) 1968
Ronnie Ray Smith (USA) 1968
Charlie Greene (USA) 1968
Eddie Hart (USA) 1972
Rey Robinson (USA) 1972
Steve Williams (USA) 1974
Silvio Leonard (Cub) 1975
Reggie Jones (USA) 1975

Electrically timed
9.95 Jim Hines (USA) 1968
10.02 Charles Greene (USA) 1968
10.04 Lennox Miller (Jam) 1968
10.05 Bob Hayes (USA) 1964
10.05 Steve Riddick (USA) 1975
10.07 Valeriy Borzov (URS) 1975

(E) 10.0
Armin Hary (Ger) 1960
Roger Bambuck (Fra) 1968
Vladislav Sapeya (URS) 1968
Valeriy Borzov (URS) 1969
Gerd Metz (Ger) 1970
Manfred Kokot (GDR) 1971
Vasilios Papageorgopoulos (Gre) 1972
Pietro Mennea (Ita) 1972
Raimo Vilen (Fin) 1972
Aleksandr Kornelyuk (URS) 1973
Michael Droese (GDR) 1973
Hans-Jurgen Bombach (GDR) 1973
Siegfried Schenke (GDR) 1973

Electrically timed
10.07 Manfred Ommer (Ger) 1974
Valeriy Borzov (URS) 1975

(C) 10.0 Pietro Mennea (Ita) 1975

(UK) 10.1
Valeriy Borzov (URS) 1975
Harry Jerome (Can) 1960
Lennox Miller (Jam) 1968
Don Quarrie (Jam) 1974
Brian Green 1972

100 YARDS

(W) 9.0
Ivory Crockett (USA) 1974
Houston McTear (USA) 1975

(E) 9.2
Chris Garpenborg (Swe) 1974
Manfred Ommer (Ger) 1974

(C) 9.1 Harry Jerome (Can) 1966
(UK) 9.4 Peter Radford 1960

200 METRES

(W) 19.8
Tommie Smith (USA) 1968
Don Quarrie (Jam) 1971

(E) 20.0 Valeriy Borzov (URS) 1972
(C) 19.8 Don Quarrie (Jam) 1971
(UK) 20.3 David Jenkins 1972

Electrically timed
19.83 Tommie Smith (USA) 1968
19.86 Don Quarrie (Jam) 1971
19.91 John Carlos (USA) 1968
20.00 Valeriy Borzov (URS) 1972
20.05 Peter Norman (Aus) 1968
20.16 Steve Williams (USA) 1975

220 YARDS	
(W) 20.0	Tommie Smith (USA) 1966
(E) 20.5	Peter Radford (UK) 1960
(C) 20.2	Carl Lawson (Jam) 1973
	Don Quarrie (Jam) 1973
400 METRES	
(W) 43.8	Lee Evans (USA) 1968
(E) 44.7	Karl Honz (Ger) 1972
(C) 44.94	Julius Sang (Ken) 1972
(UK) 44.93	David Jenkins 1975
440 YARDS	
(W) 44.5	John Smith (USA) 1971
(E) 45.9	Robbie Brightwell (UK) 1962
(C) 45.2	Wendell Mottley (Tri) 1966
800 METRES	
(W, E) 1:43.7	Marcello Fiasconaro (Ita) 1973
1:43.8	Mike Boit (Ken) 1975
(UK) 1:45.1	Andy Carter 1973
880 YARDS	
(W) 1:44.1	Rick Wohlhuter (USA) 1974
(E) 1:46.7	Jozef Plachy (Tch) 1970
(C) 1:45.1	Peter Snell (NZL) 1962
(UK) 1:47.2	Chris Carter 1968
1,000 METRES	
(W) 2:13.9	Rick Wohlhuter (USA) 1974
(E) 2:16.2	Jurgen May (GDR) 1965
	Franz-Josef Kemper (Ger) 1966
(C) 2:16.4	Mike Boit (Ken) 1973
(UK) 2:18.2	John Boulter 1969
1,500 METRES	
(W, C) 3:32.2	Filbert Bayi (Tan) 1974
(E) 3:34.0	Jean Wadoux (Fra) 1970
(UK) 3:37.4	Frank Clement 1974
MILE	
(W) 3:49	John Walker (NZL) 1975
(E) 3:53.3	Eamonn Coughlan (Irl) 1975
(C) 3:52.0	Ben Jipcho (Ken) 1973
(UK) 3:55.0	Frank Clement 1975
2,000 METRES	
(W, E) 4:56.2	Michel Jazy (Fra) 1966
(C) 5:03.2	Dave Bedford (UK) 1972
3,000 METRES	
(W, E, C) 7:35.2	Brendan Foster (UK) 1974
2 MILES	
(W, E, C) 8:13.8	Brendan Foster (UK) 1973
3 MILES	
(W, E) 12:47.8	Emiel Puttemans (Bel) 1972
(C) 12:50.4	Ron Clarke (Aus) 1966
(UK) 12:58.2	Dave Bedford 1971
5,000 METRES	
(W, E) 13:13.0	Emiel Puttemans (Bel) 1972
(C) 13:14.4	Ben Jipcho (Ken) 1974
(UK) 13:14.6	Brendan Foster 1974
6 MILES	
(W, C) 26:47.0	Ron Clarke (Aus) 1965
(E) 26:51.6	Dave Bedford (UK) 1971
10,000 METRES	
(W, E, C) 27:30.8	Dave Bedford (UK) 1973

10 MILES	
(W, E) 45:57.6	Jos Hermans (Hol) 1975
(C) 46:37.4	Jerome Drayton (Can) 1970
(UK) 46:44.0	Ron Hill 1968

20,000 METRES	
(W, E) 57:44.4	Gaston Roelants (Bel) 1972
(C) 58:39.0	Ron Hill (UK) 1968

1 HOUR	
(W, E) 20,907m	Jos Hermans (Hol) 1975
(C) 20,472m	Ron Hill (UK) 1968

15 MILES	
(W, E) 1:11:52.6	Pekka Paivarinta (Fin) 1975
(C) 1:12:48.2	Ron Hill (UK) 1965

25,000 METRES	
(W, E) 1:14:16.8	Pekka Paivarinta (Fin) 1975
(C) 1:15:22.6	Ron Hill (UK) 1965

30,000 METRES	
(W, E, C) 1:31:30.4	Jim Alder (UK) 1970

MARATHON (Best Performances)	
(W, C) 2:08:34	Derek Clayton (Aus) 1969
(E) 2:09:12	Ian Thompson (UK) 1974

3,000 METRES STEEPLECHASE	
(W, E) 8:09.8	Anders Garderud (Swe) 1975
(C) 8:14.0	Ben Jipcho (Ken) 1973
(UK) 8:22.6	John Davies 1974

120 YARDS HURDLES	
(W) 13.0	Rod Milburn (USA) 1971-73
	Guy Drut (Fra) 1975
(E) 13.0	Guy Drut (Fra) 1975
(C) 13.4	Danny Smith (Bah) 1974
(UK) 13.5	Berwyn Price 1973

110 METRES HURDLES	
(W, E) 13.0	Guy Drut (Fra) 1975
(C) 13.5	Berwyn Price (UK) 1973

200 METRES HURDLES	
(W) 22.5	Martin Lauer (Ger) 1959
	Glenn Davis (USA) 1960
(E) 22.5	Martin Lauer (Ger) 1959
(C) 22.7	Jim McCann (Aus) 1966
(UK) 23.0	Alan Pascoe 1969

400 METRES HURDLES	
(W, C) 47.8	John Akii-Bua (Uga) 1972
(E) 48.1	David Hemery (UK) 1968

440 YARDS HURDLES	
(W) 48.7	Jim Bolding (USA) 1974
(E) 49.4	Miroslav Kodejs (Tch) 1974
(C) 49.7	Gert Potgieter (SA) 1958
(UK) 50.2	David Hemery 1968

HIGH JUMP	
(W) 2.30m	Dwight Stones (USA) 1973
(E) 2.28m	Valeriy Brumel (URS) 1963
(C) 2.24m	John Beers (Can) 1973
(UK) 2.14m	Angus McKenzie 1975
	Mike Butterfield 1975

POLE VAULT	
(W) 5.65m	David Roberts (USA) 1975
5.60m	Wlad Kozakiewicz (Pol) 1975
(C) 5.34m	Kirk Bryde (Can) 1972
(UK) 5.25m	Mike Bull 1973

Previous page: The courage and athleticism of Olga Korbut (above) versus the grace and perfection of Ludmilla Turischeva (below).

Above: 'Hot' Rod Milburn (USA) defeating Guy Drut (France) to take the 1972 Olympic title in the 110m hurdles. Left: John Akii-Bua (Uganda), heir to Britain's David Hemery, taking the Olympic 400m hurdles title in a new world record time of 47.82.

LONG JUMP
(W) 8.90m   Bob Beamon (USA) 1968
(E) 8.45m   Nenad Stekić (Yug) 1975
(C) 8.23m   Lynn Davies (UK) 1968

TRIPLE JUMP
(W) 17.89m   Joao Oliveira (Bra) 1975
(E) 17.44m   Viktor Saneyev (URS) 1972
(C) 17.02m   Phil May (Aus) 1968
(UK) 16.46m Fred Alsop 1964

SHOT
(W) 21.82m   Al Feuerbach (USA) 1973
(E) 21.70m   Aleksandr Barysnikov (URS) 1974
(C) 21.37m   Geoffrey Capes (UK) 1974

DISCUS
(W) 69.10m   John Powell (USA) 1975
(E) 68.40m   Ricky Bruch (Swe) 1972
(C) 65.32m   Bishop Dolegiewicz (Can) 1975
(UK) 64.94m Bill Tancred 1974

HAMMER
(W, E) 78.50m   Karl-Heinz Riehm (Ger) 1975
(W, E) 79.30m   Walter Schmidt (Ger) 1975
(awaiting ratification)
(C) 71.26m   Barry Williams (UK) 1973

JAVELIN
(W, E) 94.08m   Klaus Wolfermann (Ger) 1973
(C) 84.92m   Charles Clover (UK) 1974

DECATHLON
(W) 8,524   Bruce Jenner (USA) 1975
(E) 8,454   Nikolay Avilov (URS) 1972
(C) 7,903   Peter Gabbett (UK) 1971

4 x 100 METRES RELAY
(W) 38.2   USA 1968-72
(E) 38.4   France 1968
(C) 38.3   Jamaica 1968
(UK) 39.3   National Team 1968

4 x 110 YARDS RELAY
(W) 38.6   Univ. of S. California 1967
(E) 39.5   West Germany 1975
(C) 39.8   Ghana 1966

4 x 200 METRES RELAY
(W, E) 1:21.5   Italy 1972
(C) 1:22.5   Trinidad and Tobago 1972
(UK) 1:24.1   National Team 1971

4 x 220 YARDS RELAY
(W) 1:21.5   Texas A and M University 1970

4 x 400 METRES RELAY
(W) 2:56.1   USA 1968
(E) 3:00.5   West Germany 1968
             Poland 1968
             United Kingdom 1972
(C) 2:59.6   Kenya 1968

4 x 440 YARDS RELAY
(W, C) 3:02.8   Trinidad and Tobago 1966
(E) 3:03.2   West Germany 1975
(UK) 3:06.5   England 1966

4 x 800 METRES RELAY
(W, E) 7:08.6   West Germany 1966
(C) 7:11.6   Kenya 1970
(UK) 7:17.4   National Team 1970

4 x 880 YARDS RELAY
(W) 7:10.4 — Univ. of Chicago TC 1973
(E) 7:14.6 — West Germany 1968
(C) 7:11.6 — Kenya 1970
(UK) 7:17.4 — National Team 1970

4 x 1,500 METRES RELAY
(W, C) 14:40.4 — New Zealand 1973
(E) 14:49.0 — France 1965
(UK) 15:06.6 — National Team 1971

4 x MILE RELAY
(W, C) 16:02.8 — New Zealand 1972
(E) 16:09.6 — West Germany 1969
(UK) 16:24.8 — Northern Counties 1961

ONE HOUR WALK
(C) 13,960m — Phil Embleton (UK) 1972

10 MILES WALK
(C) 1:09:40.6 — Ken Matthews (UK) 1964

20,000 METRES WALK
(W, E) 1:24:45.0 — Bernd Kannenberg (Ger) 1974
(C) 1:28:45.8 — Ken Matthews (UK) 1964

2 HOURS WALK
(W, E) 27,154m — Bernd Kannenberg (Ger) 1974
(C) 26,118m — Ted Allsopp (Aus) 1956
(UK) 26,037m — Ron Wallwork 1971

30,000 METRES WALK
(W, E) 2:12:58.0 — Bernd Kannenberg (Ger) 1974
(C) 2:24:18.2 — Roy Thorpe (UK) 1974

20 MILES WALK
(W, E) 2:30:38.6 — Gerhard Weidner (Ger) 1974
(C) 2:34:25.4 — John Warhurst (UK) 1974

30 MILES WALK
(W, E) 3:51:48.6 — Gerhard Weidner (Ger) 1973
(C) 4:02:49.2 — Bob Dobson (UK) 1974

50 KILOMETRES WALK
(W, E) 4:00:27.2 — Gerhard Weidner (Ger) 1973
(C) 4:11:22.0 — Bob Dobson (UK) 1974

WOMEN
60 METRES
(W) 7.2 — Betty Cuthbert (Aus) 1960 / Irina Bochkaryova (URS) 1960 / Andrea Lynch (UK) 1974 / Lea Allaerts (Bel) 1975
(E) 7.2 — Irina Bochkaryova (URS) 1960 / Andrea Lynch (UK) 1974 / Lea Allaerts (Bel) 1975
(C) 7.2 — Betty Cuthbert (Aus) 1960 / Andrea Lynch (UK) 1974

100 YARDS
(W) 10.0 — Chi Cheng (Tai) 1970
(E) 10.6 — Heather Young (UK) 1958 / Dorothy Hyman (UK) 1962-64 / Mary Rand (UK) 1964 / Daphne Arden (UK) 1964 / Marlene Willard (Aus) 1958
(C) 10.3

100 METRES
(W, E) 10.8 — Renate Stecher (GDR) 1973 / Raelene Boyle (Aus) 1968-71 / Alice Annum (Gha) 1971
(C) 11.1 — Andrea Lynch (UK) 1974

Fully automatic timing:
(W, E) 11.07 — Renate Stecher (GDR) 1972
(UK) 11.16 — Andrea Lynch 1975

Above: New Zealander John Walker has made an onslaught on the one mile world record which has meant an improvement of 10 seconds since Roger Bannister first shattered the four-minute mile in 1954. Above right: One of the closest margins of victory in the Munich Olympics was that of Klaus Wolfermann (West Germany) over Janis Lusis of the USSR in the javelin. Wolfermann went on to set a new world record and should be in Montreal to defend his title. Right: The greatest all-round woman athlete in the world, Irena Szewinska of Poland.

200 METRES
(W, E) 22.0
(C) 22.5
(UK) 23.0
Irena Szewinska (Pol) 1974
Raelene Boyle (Aus) 1972-74
Helen Golden 1974

220 YARDS
(W) 22.6
(E) 22.7
(C) 22.9
(UK) 23.6
Chi Cheng (Tai) 1970
Renate Stecher (GDR) 1975
Margaret Burvill (Aus) 1964
Daphne Arden 1964

400 METRES
(W, E) 49.9
(C) 51.0
(UK) 51.28
Fully automatic timing:
(W, E) 50.14
Irena Szewinska (Pol) 1974
Marilyn Neufville (Jam) 1970
Donna Murray 1975

440 YARDS
(W) 52.2

(E) 53.7
(C) 52.4
(UK) 54.1
Rita Salin (Fin) 1974

800 METRES
(W, E) 1:57.5
(C) 2:00.1
(UK) 2:00.2
Kathy Hammond (USA) 1972
Debra Sapenter (USA) 1974
Maria Itkina (URS) 1959
Judy Pollock (Aus) 1965
Deirdre Watkinson 1966

880 YARDS
(W, C) 2:02.0

(E) 2:03.0
(UK) 2:04.2
Svetla Zlateva (Bul) 1973
Yvonne Saunders (Can) 1975
Rosemary Stirling 1972

Dixie Willis (Aus) 1962
Judy Pollock (Aus) 1967
Vera Nikolic (Yug) 1967
Anne Smith 1966

1,500 METRES
(W, E) 4:01.4
(C) 4:04.8
Ludmila Bragina (URS) 1972
Sheila Carey (UK) 1972

MILE
(W, E) 4:29.5
(C) 4:34.9
(UK) 4:36.2
Paola Cacchi (Ita) 1973
Glenda Reiser (Can) 1973
Joan Allison 1973

3,000 METRES
(W, E) 8:46.6
(C) 8:55.6
Greta Anderson (Nor) 1975
Joyce Smith (UK) 1974

100 METRES HURDLES
(W, E) 12.3
(C) 12.5
(UK) 13.0
Annelie Ehrhardt (GDR) 1973
Pam Ryan (Aus) 1972
Judy Vernon 1974
Blondelle Thompson 1974

400 METRES HURDLES
(W, E) 56.5
(C) 58.0
Krystyna Kacperczyk (Pol) 1974
Christine Warden (UK) 1974

HIGH JUMP
(W, E) 1.95m
(C) 1.89m
Rosemarie Witschas (GDR) 1974
Debbie Brill (Can) 1975

LONG JUMP
(W, E) 6.84m
(C) 6.76m
Heide Rosendahl (Ger) 1970
Mary Rand (UK) 1964

SHOT
(W, E) 21.60m
(C) 17.26m
(UK) 16.31m
Marianne Adam (GDR) 1975
Val Young (NZL) 1964
Mary Peters (UK) 1966

DISCUS
(W, E) 70.20m   Faina Melnik (URS) 1975
(C) 58.02m   Rosemary Payne (UK) 1972

JAVELIN
(W, E) 67.22m   Ruth Fuchs (GDR) 1974
(C) 62.24m   Petra Rivers (Aus) 1972
(UK) 55.60m   Sue Platt 1968

PENTATHLON
(W, E) 4932   Burglinde Pollak (GDR) 1973
(C) 4801   Mary Peters (UK) 1972

4 x 110 YARDS RELAY
(W, E) 44.1   West Germany 1975
(C) 45.0   United Kingdom 1968

4 x 200 METRES RELAY
(W, E, C) 1:33.8   United Kingdom 1968

4 x 220 YARDS RELAY
(W, C) 1:35.8   Australia 1969
(E) 1:36.0   East Germany 1958

4 x 400 METRES RELAY
(W, E) 3:23.0   East Germany 1972
(C) 3:28.7   United Kingdom 1972

4 x 440 YARDS RELAY
(W, E) 3:30.3   West Germany 1975

4 x 800 METRES RELAY
(W, E) 8:05.2   Bulgaria 1975
(C) 8:23.8   United Kingdom 1971

MILE WALK
(UK) 7:36.2   Judy Farr 1965

3,000 METRES WALK
(UK) 14:33.6   Marion Fawkes 1974

5,000 METRES WALK
(UK) 24:59.2   Marion Fawkes 1974

4 x 100 METRES RELAY
(W, E) 42.5   East Germany 1974
(C) 43.4   Australia 1968
(UK) 43.7   National Team 1968-72

SWIMMING AND DIVING

In the Munich Olympics every single Olympic swimming record was smashed, and in Montreal the story will be repeated, though Mark Spitz's 100m butterfly record may well remain unbeaten. Once again the powerful United States should dominate the men's swimming, as they have since the Tokyo Olympics in 1964. The men's freestyle events should all go to the US together with the butterfly and possibly the backstroke. In the breaststroke, Britain's David Wilkie could resist the challenge of world record holder John Hencken of the US and win both the 100m and 200m events. No male swimmer will be able to emulate Mark Spitz and win seven gold medals; the highest possible number would be three by either Tim Shaw or John Naber, both of the US.

There is a different story in the women's events. Kornelia Ender will lead East Germany's challenge and could win five gold medals (100 and 200m freestyle, 100m butterfly, 4 x 100m medley team, 4 x 100m freestyle team). East Germany will dominate in the women's swimming even more than the US in the men's. Australia, once the world's swimming nation, have slipped back, but they could still win medals in the distance freestyle events.

Olympic swimming always seems to produce some surprises. In Munich we had Nobutaka Taguchi and Mayumi Aoki, both gold medallists for Japan, and in 1976 it is likely that Canada will do very well indeed. The Canadians have given great encouragement to their swimmers over the past four years and have been guided by two great coaches, Deryk Snelling of Great Britain and Don Talbot of Australia.

Great Britain could have its most successful Olympic Games since 1908 if the men can recapture their 1975 World Championship form. David Wilkie and Brian Brinkley are both outstanding prospects and will add their strength to the team events, in which Great Britain could well win the silver medal.

Men's events

100m freestyle The US have tremendous depth in all freestyle events and have the favourites for the gold medal in world record holder Jim Montgomery and fellow American Andy Coan. Together with Bruce Furness, also of the US, they could make a clean sweep of the medals, although 1972 bronze medallist Vladimir Bure (USSR), the European record holder, could cause an upset if he can increase his stamina. Look out also for three more Europeans, Peter Nocke and Klaus Steinbach, both of West Germany, and the fast-improving

Previous page: Rosemary Kother (top) of East Germany captured the world title for the 200m butterfly in both 1973 and 1975 and is a strong favourite for the gold medal in Montreal. Andy Coan (middle) of the US is 1975 World Champion in the 100m freestyle. In Montreal he is expected to have a tough battle against fellow countryman Jim Montgomery, current world record holder.

Jenny Turrall (bottom) of Australia is World Champion and record holder for the 800m freestyle event, and a likely gold medallist in Montreal, though she may have tough competition from Shirley Babashoff of the US. Her chances will also be excellent in the 400m freestyle if she can improve her basic speed.

100 METRES FREESTYLE (Men)

Munich 1972		World Championships — Cali 1975	
1. Mark Spitz (USA)	51.22	1. Andy Coan (USA)	51.25
2. Jerry Heidenreich (USA)	51.65	2. Vladimir Bure (URS)	51.32
3. Vladimir Bure (URS)	51.77	3. James Montgomery (USA)	51.44
4. John Murphy (USA)	52.08	4. Peter Nocke (Ger)	52.15
5. Mike Wenden (Aus)	52.41	5. Klaus Steinbach (Ger)	52.20
6. Igor Grivennikov (URS)	52.44	6. Marcello Guarducci (Ita)	52.55

200 METRES FREESTYLE (Men)

Munich 1972		World Championships — Cali 1975	
1. Mark Spitz (USA)	1:52.78	1. Tim Shaw (USA)	1:51.04
2. Steve Genter (USA)	1:53.73	2. Bruce Furness (USA)	1:51.72
3. Werner Lampe (Ger)	1:53.99	3. Brian Brinkley (GBR)	1:53.56
4. Mike Wenden (Aus)	1:54.40	4. Andrei Krylov (URS)	1:54.23
5. Fred Tyler (USA)	1:54.96	5. Peter Nocke (Ger)	1:54.81
6. Klaus Steinbach (Ger)	1:55.65	6. Gordon Downie (GBR)	1:55.08

young Italian Marcello Guarducci.

200m freestyle The world record set by Mark Spitz in Munich has been shattered. Bruce Furness and Tim Shaw, both of the US, will fight it out for the gold medal, with the edge going to Furness. However, Britain's Brian Brinkley, third in Cali in 1975 with a vastly improved speed, could cause a real upset. Gordon Downie of Great Britain who was sixth in Cali is still improving; he will be looking for a place in the final in Montreal. Watch for the impressively smooth techniques which characterize the US team.

400m freestyle Since Munich, the 400m freestyle record has been reduced by nearly 7 seconds. Once again the US should dominate; they are favourites to take all three medals. World Champion and record holder Tim Shaw, together with Bruce Furness and Brian Goodall, is far ahead of the rest of the world. In fact, the US have 16 swimmers in the 1975 top 20 world rankings! However, British swimmers Brian Brinkley and Gordon Downie will be aiming to reach the final, and if they do they will have an outside chance.

400 METRES FREESTYLE (Men)

Munich 1972		World Championships — Cali 1975	
1. Bradford Cooper (Aus)	4:00.27	1. Tim Shaw (USA)	3:54.88
2. Steve Genter (USA)	4:01.94	2. Bruce Furness (USA)	3:57.71
3. Tom McBreen (USA)	4:02.64	3. Frank Pfutze (GDR)	4:01.10
4. Graham Windeatt (Aus)	4:02.93	4. Graham Windeatt (Aus)	4:02.72
5. Brian Brinkley (GBR)	4:06.69	5. Gordon Downie (GBR)	4:02.88
6. Bengt Gingsjoe (Swe)	4:06.75	6. Rainer Strobach (GDR)	4:05.19

1,500 METRES FREESTYLE (Men)

Munich 1972		World Championships — Cali 1975	
1. Mike Burton (USA)	15:52.58	1. Tim Shaw (USA)	15:28.92
2. Graham Windeatt (Aus)	15:58.48	2. Brian Goodell (USA)	15:39.00
3. Douglas Northway (USA)	16.09.25	3. David Parker (GBR)	15:58.21
4. Bengt Gingsjoe (Swe)	16:16.01	4. Frank Pfutze (GDR)	16:05.32
5. Graham White (Aus)	16:17.22	5. Rainer Strobach (GDR)	16:09.75
6. Mark Treffers (NZL)	16:18.84	6. Mark Treffers (NZL)	16:11.17

1,500m freestyle With fast-starting world record holder Tim Shaw (US) fighting off Steve Holland, the fast-finishing Australian, the 1,500m freestyle will be one of the most interesting tactical races of the Olympic swimming programme. Speeds in distance events have become very much faster over the past four years and the Olympic record held by Mike Burton of the US will be shattered by up to 40 seconds in Montreal! The winner could come from any three US swimmers, but my favourite is Steve Holland of Australia. Watch for Britain's European silver medallist Jim Carter, and David Parker, who won the bronze medal in Cali. Both swimmers could spring a surprise.

100 METRES BUTTERFLY (Men)

Munich 1972		World Championships — Cali 1975	
1. Mark Spitz (USA)	54.27	1. Greg Jagenburg (USA)	55.63
2. Bruce Robertson (Can)	55.56	2. Roger Pyttel (GDR)	56.04
3. Jerry Heidenreich (USA)	55.74	3. Bill Forrester (USA)	56.07
4. Roland Matthes (GDR)	55.87	4. Bruce Robertson (Can)	56.39
5. David Edgar (USA)	56.11	5. Jorge Delgado (Ecu)	56.66
6. Byron MacDonald (Can)	57.27	6. Brian Brinkley (GBR)	56.68

100m butterfly This event was Mark Spitz's best and no one has yet had enough speed and technique to approach his Olympic world record. The competition for all places in the final will be hotly contested, with no really outstanding favourite for the gold medal. Any one of the three US swimmers who qualify for their Olympic team, plus Canada's Bruce Robertson, Britain's Brian Brinkley and East Germany's very talented Roger Pyttel should share the first six places, with the gold medal going to the fastest finisher — who could be Mike Bottom of the US.

200m butterfly Brian Brinkley of Great Britain and Roger Pyttel of East Germany pose the biggest threat to US domination of this event. Greg Jagenburg (US) failed in 1975 to break Mark Spitz's record by 7/100ths of a second and he and World Champion Bill Forrester look like the ones to beat. Brinkley, if he can continue his great

Munich 1972		World Championships — Cali 1975	
1. Mark Spitz (USA)	2:00.70	1. Bill Forrester (USA)	2:01.95
2. Garry Hall (USA)	2:02.86	2. Roger Pyttel (GDR)	2:02.22
3. Robin Backhaus (USA)	2:03.23	3. Brian Brinkley (GBR)	2:02.45
4. Jorge Delgado (Ecu)	2:04.60	4. Greg Jagenburg (USA)	2:02.97
5. Hans Fassnacht (Ger)	2:04.69	5. Jorge Delgado (Ecu)	2:03.18
6. Andras Hargitay (Hun)	2:04.69	6. Michael Kraus (Ger)	2:03.47

improvement, could surprise everyone. The winning time is certain to be under the 2 minute barrier.

100m breaststroke Britain's David Wilkie, the World, European and Commonwealth Champion will renew his rivalry with world record holder John Hencken of the US. Wilkie is still developing his speed and strength while Hencken has not improved for a year. David Leigh, also of Great Britain, has the speed to upset them both but needs to improve his staying power. Taguchi of Japan, the Olympic Champion, and Pankin of the USSR will be fighting for the bronze, together with the 'dark horse', Walter Kusch of West Germany.

200m breaststroke Only 2/100ths of a second separate Wilkie of Great Britain and Hencken of the US but my favourite is Wilkie. He won the world title in Cali with a time of 2.18.23 but he had no real opposition and was swimming at a high altitude. He should improve on that time considerably in Montreal to bring home the gold. Third place should be a battle between David Leigh of Great Britain, Colella of the US, Pankin of the USSR and Kusch of West Germany.

100 METRES BREASTSTROKE (Men)

Munich 1972		World Championships — Cali 1975	
1. Nobutaka Taguchi (Jpn)	64.94	1. David Wilkie (GBR)	64.26
2. Tom Bruce (USA)	65.43	2. Nobutaka Taguchi (Jpn)	65.04
3. John Hencken (USA)	65.61	3. David Leigh (GBR)	65.32
4. Mark Chatfield (USA)	66.01	4. Rick Colella (USA)	65.56
5. Walter Kusch (Ger)	66.23	5. Nicolai Pankin (URS)	65.71
6. Jose Fiolo (Bra)	66.24	6. Walter Kusch (Ger)	65.76

200 METRES BREASTSTROKE (Men)

Munich 1972		World Championships — Cali 1975	
1. John Hencken (USA)	2:21.55	1. David Wilkie (GBR)	2:18.23
2. David Wilkie (GBR)	2:23.67	2. Rick Colella (USA)	2:21.60
3. Nobutaka Taguchi (Jpn)	2:23.88	3. Nicolai Pankin (URS)	2:21.75
4. Rick Colella (USA)	2:24.28	4. Walter Kusch (Ger)	2:22.68
5. Felipe Munoz (Mex)	2:26.44	5. David Leigh (GBR)	2:23.38
6. Walter Kusch (Ger)	2:26.55	6. Nobutaka Taguchi (Jpn)	2:24.08

100m backstroke The men's backstroke races will provide some of the most interesting in the programme, involving literally the giants of world swimming. Will the twenty-six-year-old Olympic Champion, 6ft 3in Roland Matthes of East Germany be able to fight off the challenge from 6ft 6in John Naber of the US and 6ft 5in Steve Pickell of Canada? Also in the running might be 6ft 5in John Murphy of the US, 1972 bronze medallist, Australia's fast-improving Mark Tonelli and 6ft 5in Lutz Wanja of East Germany.

200m backstroke Big John Naber of the US is clear favourite for this event. He is almost two seconds clear in the 1975 world rankings over fellow US swimmers Dan Harrigan and Bruce Hardcastle. The only two non-US swimmers who could cause an upset are World Champion Zoltan Verraszto of Hungary and Australia's Mark Tonelli, whom I rate very highly indeed. Defending Champion Roland Matthes seems to have lost his zest for this event; he finished a poor fourth in Cali. Great Britain's Jim Carter should make the final if he decides to swim this event, but at present he does not have the basic speed to upset the favourites.

100 METRES BACKSTROKE (Men)

Munich 1972		*World Championships — Cali 1975*	
1. Roland Matthes (GDR)	56.58	1. Roland Matthes (GDR)	58.15
2. Mike Stamm (USA)	57.70	2. John Murphy (USA)	58.34
3. John Murphy (USA)	58.35	3. Mel Nash (USA)	58.38
4. Mitch Ivey (USA)	58.48	4. Lutz Wanja (GDR)	58.43
5. Igor Grivennikov (URS)	59.50	5. Steve Pickell (Can)	58.63
6. Lutz Wanja (GDR)	59.80	6. Mark Tonelli (Aus)	58.72

200 METRES BACKSTROKE (Men)

Munich 1972		*World Championships — Cali 1975*	
1. Roland Matthes (GDR)	2:02.82	1. Zoltan Verraszto (Hun)	2:05.06
2. Mike Stamm (USA)	2:04.09	2. Mark Tonelli (Aus)	2:05.78
3. Mitch Ivey (USA)	2:04.33	3. Paul Hore (USA)	2:06.49
4. Brad Cooper (Aus)	2:06.59	4. Roland Matthes (GDR)	2:07.09
5. Tim McKee (USA)	2:07.29	5. Zoltan Rudolf (Hun)	2:07.15
6. Lothar Noack (GDR)	2:08.67	6. Santiago Esteva (Esp)	2:09.21

400m individual medley Gunnar Larsson of Sweden won the Olympic title in 1972 by 2/100ths of a second over Tim McKee of the US. However, world record holder and World Champion Andras Hargity of Hungary is unbeaten in this event for the past three years and should win comfortably in Montreal. Steve Furness and Dave Hannula, both of the US, look likely to take the silver and bronze, but

400 METRES INDIVIDUAL MEDLEY (Men)

Munich 1972		World Championships — Cali 1975	
1. Gunnar Larsson (Swe)	4:31.98	1. Andras Hargitay (Hun)	4:32.57
2. Tim McKee (USA)	4:31.98	2. Andrei Smirnov (URS)	4:35.63
3. Andras Hargitay (Hun)	4:32.70	3. Hans Geisler (Ger)	4:36.40
4. Steve Furness (USA)	4:35.44	4. Dave Hannula (USA)	4:36.52
5. Gary Hall (USA)	4:37.38	5. Jim Fowlie (Can)	4:38.02
6. Bengt Gingsjoe (Swe)	4:37.96	6. Jim Carter (GBR)	4:39.30

4 x 100 METRES MEDLEY RELAY (Men)

Munich 1972		World Championships — Cali 1975	
1. USA	3:48.16	1. USA	3:49.00
2. GDR	3:52.12	2. Ger	3:51.85
3. Can	3:52.26	3. GBR	3:52.80
4. URS	3:53.26	4. Can	3:53.88
5. Bra	3:57.89	5. GDR	3:55.44
6. Jpn	3:58.23	6. URS	3:55.84

they will have to watch Canada's Jim Fowlie and the USSR's Andrei
Smirnov. Jim Carter and Alan McClatchey of Great Britain could both
make the final in what could be one of the most exciting races in
Montreal.

4 x 100m medley relay (backstroke, breaststroke, butterfly, freestyle)
The US, with their tremendous strength in depth, will easily win the
gold medal in this event unless there is a disqualification. The silver
and bronze medals will be hotly contested by West Germany,
Great Britain and Canada. Great Britain have a great chance for the
silver if they can improve on their backstroke leg.

4 x 200m freestyle relay The overwhelming depth of talent on
freestyle in the US is demonstrated by the fact that the Long Beach
Swim Club team holds the world record. In the 1975 World
Championships the US were disqualified, but that is unlikely to
happen in Montreal. Great Britain, West Germany and the USSR will
battle for silver and bronze.

4 x 200 METRES FREESTYLE RELAY (Men)

Munich 1972		World Championships — Cali 1975	
1. USA	7:35.78	1. Ger	7:39.44
2. Ger	7:41.69	2. GBR	7:42.55
3. URS	7:45.76	3. URS	7:43.58
4. Swe	7:47.37	4. Swe	7:47.05
5. Aus	7:48.66	5. GDR	7:52.24
6. GDR	7:49.11	6. Can	7:53.21

Women's events

100m freestyle East Germany's Kornelia Ender looks certain to win the gold medal. However, Enith Brigitha of Holland could come close if she can reproduce her relay form at Cali. Second and third places are wide open, but watch for Barbara Krause of East Germany, who has a 57.5 timing to her credit. It will take a 58.5 or thereabouts to make the final.

200m freestyle Shirley Babashoff of the US and Kornelia Ender of East Germany are the World Champion and world record holder respectively; they look set to repeat the race they had in Cali. If Kornelia Ender paces her race more intelligently she could win easily, for she has far superior speed. Enith Brigitha of Holland or Kim Peyton

100 METRES FREESTYLE (Women)

Munich 1972		*World Championships — Cali 1975*	
1. Sandra Neilson (USA)	58.59	1. Kornelia Ender (GDR)	56.50
2. Shirley Babashoff (USA)	59.02	2. Shirley Babashoff (USA)	57.81
3. Shane Gould (Aus)	59.06	3. Enith Brigitha (Hol)	58.20
4. Gabriele Wetzko (GDR)	59.21	4. Kathy Heddy (USA)	58.21
5. Heidmarie Reineck (Ger)	59.73	5. Barbara Krause (GDR)	58.22
6. Andrea Eife (GDR)	59.91	6. Jutta Weber (Ger)	58.33

200 METRES FREESTYLE (Women)

Munich 1972		*World Championships — Cali 1975*	
1. Shane Gould (Aus)	2:03.56	1. Shirley Babashoff (USA)	2:02.50
2. Shirley Babashoff (USA)	2:04.33	2. Kornelia Ender (GDR)	2:02.69
3. Keena Rothhammer (USA)	2:04.92	3. Enith Brigitha (Hol)	2:03.92
4. Ann Marshall (USA)	2:05.45	4. Valerie Lee (USA)	2:04.15
5. Andrea Eife (GDR)	2:06.27	5. Sonya Gray (Aus)	2:05.16
6. Hansje Bunschoten (Hol)	2:08.40	6. Gail Amundrud (Can)	2:05.58

400 METRES FREESTYLE (Women)

Munich 1972		*World Championships — Cali 1975*	
1. Shane Gould (Aus)	4:19.04	1. Shirley Babashoff (USA)	4:16.87
2. Novella Calligaris (Ita)	4:22.44	2. Jenny Turrall (Aus)	4:17.88
3. Gudrun Wegner (GDR)	4:23.11	3. Kathy Heddy (USA)	4:18.03
4. Shirley Babashoff (USA)	4:23.59	4. Sabine Kahle (GDR)	4:20.27
5. Jennie Wylie (USA)	4:24.07	5. Sonya Gray (USA)	4:23.72
6. K. Rothhammer (USA)	4:24.22	6. Gail Amundrud (Can)	4:23.99

of the US could win the bronze, but Canada's Gail Amundrud could also do well.

400m freestyle World record holder and World Champion Shirley Babashoff could win her second gold medal in this event, but she will have to overcome a strong challenge from Australians Jenny Turrall and Sonya Gray, who are both very close to the world record. Sonya Gray was ill in Cali but set a new Commonwealth record in April 1975.

800m freestyle Jenny Turrall of Australia and Heather Greenwood of the US should provide a great race in the 800m freestyle. In Cali Heather Greenwood swam too fast in the early stages of the race and was caught and passed by Jenny Turrall by the 600m mark. Shirley Babashoff of the US could spring a surprise if she manages to pace herself through the Olympic swimming programme; she certainly has far superior basic speed than either of the favourites, but will she be overtired by the time of the 800m race?

800 METRES FREESTYLE (Women)

Munich 1972		*World Championships — Cali 1975*	
1. Keena Rothhammer (USA)	8:53.68	1. Jenny Turrall (Aus)	8:44.75 (split 4:23.23)
2. Shane Gould (Aus)	8:56.39	2. Heather Greenwood (USA)	8:48.88
3. Novella Calligaris (Ita)	8:57.46		(split 4:20.37)
4. Ann Simmons (USA)	8:57.62	3. Shirley Babashoff (USA)	8:53.22
5. Gudrun Wegner (GDR)	8:58.89	4. Kornelia Doerr (GDR)	8:55.38
6. Jo Harshbarger (USA)	9:01.21	5. R. Milgate (Aus)	8:55.51
		6. Sabine Kahle (GDR)	8:59.14

100 METRES BACKSTROKE (Women)

Munich 1972		*World Championships — Cali 1975*	
1. Melissa Belote (USA)	1:05.78	1. Ulrike Richter (GDR)	1:03.80
2. Andrea Gyarmati (Hun)	1:06.34	2. Brigit Treiber (GDR)	1:04.34
3. Susie Atwood (USA)	1:06.34	3. Nancy Garapick (Can)	1:04.73
4. Karen Moe (USA)	1:06.69	4. Wendy Cook (Can)	1:06.06
5. Wendy Cook (Can)	1:06.70	5. Linda Jezek (USA)	1:06.74
6. Enith Brigitha (Hol)	1:06.82	6. Angelika Greiser (Ger)	1:06.90

200 METRES BACKSTROKE (Women)

Munich 1972		*World Championships — Cali 1975*	
1. Melissa Belote (USA)	2:19.19	1. Brigit Treiber (GDR)	2:15.46
2. Susie Atwood (USA)	2:20.38	2. Nancy Garapick (Can)	2:16.09
3. Donna Gurr (Can)	2:23.22	3. Ulrike Richter (GDR)	2:18.76
4. Anne Kober (Ger)	2:23.35	4. Ellen Wallace (USA)	2:20.42
5. Christine Herbst (GDR)	2:23.44	5. Monique Rohdahl (NZL)	2:21.62
6. Enith Brigitha (Hol)	2:23.70	6. Starko Nadezhda (URS)	2:23.38

100m backstroke East Germany's Ulricke Richter should have no trouble in dominating this event. She is very strong, as are all the East German girls, and has far more speed than any other swimmer in the world at present. Canada's Nancy Garapick and East Germany's Brigit Treiber, the 200m World Champion and record holder, will battle for the silver and bronze.

200m backstroke Canada has a great chance for a gold medal if the diminutive Nancy Garapick of Halifax, Nova Scotia, can improve her stamina for 1976. She appeared from nowhere in 1974 and only just lost a thrilling race in the 200m event in the 1975 World Championships at Cali. Both she and World Champion Brigit Treiber of East Germany are well in front of the rest of the world. The bronze could be taken by Ulricke Richter of East Germany, 1972 Olympic Champion Melissa Belote of the US, or Canada's Cheryl Gibson.

100m breaststroke Hannelore Anke of East Germany was an easy winner in this event in the 1975 World Championships and she should have no trouble in taking the Olympic title, unless her teammate Karla

100 METRES BREASTSTROKE (Women)

Munich 1972		*World Championships — Cali 1975*	
1. Cathy Carr (USA)	1:13.58	1. Hannelore Anke (GDR)	1:12.72
2. Galina Stepanora (URS)	1:14.99	2. Widja Mazereeuw (Hol)	1:14.29
3. Beverley Whitfield (Aus)	1:15.73	3. Marcia Morey (USA)	1:15.00
4. Agnes Kaczander (Hun)	1:16.26	4. Karla Linke (GDR)	1:15.32
5. Judy Melick (USA)	1:16.34	5. Luibor Rusanore (URS)	1:15.32
6. Verena Eberle (Ger)	1:17.16	6. Gabriele Askamp (Ger)	1:15.37

200 METRES BREASTSTROKE (Women)

Munich 1972		*World Championships — Cali 1975*	
1. Beverley Whitfield (Aus)	2:41.71	1. Hannelore Anke (GDR)	2:37.25
2. Dana Schoenfield (USA)	2:42.05	2. Widja Mazereeuw (Hol)	2:37.50
3. Galina Stepanora (URS)	2:42.36	3. Karla Linke (GDR)	2:38.10
4. Claudia Clevenger (USA)	2:42.88	4. Laurie Siering (USA)	2:39.55
5. Petia Nows (Ger)	2:43.38	5. Luibor Rusanova (URS)	2:40.80
6. Agnes Kaczander (Hun)	2:43.41	6. Joanne Baker (Can)	2:42.55

Linke improves her speed dramatically. Britain's Margaret Kelly improved greatly in 1975 and has the speed to do really well, although the US swimmer Marcia Morey and Canadians Marian Stuart and Joanne Baker also pose a real threat.

200m breaststroke The Olympic breaststroke races have a record of surprises. Beverly Whitfield of Australia took the Olympic title in 1972 when Galina Stepanora of the USSR looked a certain winner, and Japan's Taguchi surprised everyone in the men's 100m. The Mexico Olympics also produced some unexpected winners in Mexico's Muroz (men's 200m) and Yugoslavia's Bjedor. There are three swimmers in the world who seem clear favourites for the medals: Anke of East Germany, Mazereeuw of Holland and world record holder Linke of East Germany. However, Canada's Joanne Baker and Britain's Margaret Kelly could do very well, as could US swimmers Morey and Siering.

100m butterfly East Germany should dominate this event and could take all three medals, with the closest challenges coming from Camille Wright and Jill Simons of the US, and Barbara Clarke of Canada. Great Britain's Anne Adams may reach the final if she can improve by at least 1.50 seconds.

200m butterfly East Germany look set to dominate this event as well as the 100m. World Champion and record holder Rosemarie Kother of East Germany has not been beaten for two years and newcomer Gabrielle Wuschek, also of East Germany, looks very strong indeed. Valerie Lee of the US should be among the medal-winners.

100 METRES BUTTERFLY (Women)

Munich 1972		*1975 World Championships — Cali 1975*	
1. Mayumi Aoki (Jpn)	1:03.34	1. Kornelia Ender (GDR)	1:01.24
2. Roswitha Beier (GDR)	1:03.61	2. Rosemarie Kother (GDR)	1:01.80
3. Andrea Gyarmati (Hun)	1:03.73	3. Camille Wright (USA)	1:02.79
4. Deena Deardurff (USA)	1:03.95	4. Jill Simons (USA)	1:03.51
5. Dana Schrader (USA)	1:03.98	5. Pavis Milagros (CRC)	1:03.86
6. Ellie Daniel (USA)	1:04.08	6. Barbara Clarke (Can)	1:04.06

200 METRES BUTTERFLY (Women)

Munich 1972		World Championships— Cali 1975	
1. Karen Moe (USA)	2:15.57	1. Rosemarie Kother (GDR)	2:13.82
2. Lyn Colella (USA)	2:16.34	2. Valerie Lee (USA)	2:14.89
3. Ellie Daniel (USA)	2:16.74	3. Gabrielle Wuschek (GDR)	2:15.96
4. Rosemarie Kother (GDR)	2:17.11	4. Camille Wright (USA)	2:17.21
5. Noviko Asano (Jpn)	2:19.50	5. Natalie Popora (URS)	2:18.31
6. Helga Lindner (GDR)	2:20.47	6. Wendy Quirk (Can)	2:18.63

400m individual medley There has been a tremendous improvement in women's medley swimming, as can be seen from the ten second difference between the Olympic and World Records. Until September 1975 Ulricke Tauber of East Germany was clearly out in front of the rest of the world by some four seconds and she was an easy winner in Cali. However, I expect the US swimmers Jenny Franks with a 4.53.86 and Kathy Heddy with a 4.53.88 to their credit in the US Championships (August 1975) to challenge Ulricke Tauber strongly. Cheryl Gibson of Canada could also be in the reckoning. Susan Richardson of Great Britain has the talent but will have to improve by some six seconds in order to reach the final, in which even the slowest qualifier will easily beat the 1972 winning time!

400 METRES INDIVIDUAL MEDLEY (Women)

Munich 1972		World Championships— Cali 1975	
1. Gail Neall (Aus)	5:02.97	1. Ulricke Tauber (GDR)	4:52.76
2. Leslie Cliff (Can)	5:03.57	2. Karla Luike (GDR)	4:57.83
3. Novella Calligaris (Ita)	5:03.99	3. Kathy Heddy (USA)	5:00.46
4. Jenny Bartz (USA)	5:05.56	4. Jenny Franks (USA)	5:03.15
5. Evlyn Stolze (GDR)	5:06.80	5. Liz McKinnon (Can)	5:03.81
6. Mary Montgomery (USA)	5:09.98	6. Susan Hunter (NZL)	5:03.85

4 x 100m medley relay The East German team, with the world record holder in each individual stroke, cannot fail to win the gold medal, unless there is a disqualification. Canada, the US, and Holland will fight it out for the silver and bronze medals.

4 x 100 METRES MEDLEY RELAY (Women)

Munich 1972		World Championships— Cali 1975	
1. USA	4:20.75	1. GDR	4:14.74
2. GDR	4:24.91	2. USA	4:20.47
3. Ger	4:26.46	3. Hol	4:21.45

4 x 100m freestyle relay In Munich this event was a very exciting

affair resulting in a narrow win for the United States over East Germany. The result was reversed in Cali and will likely be the same in Montreal. Canada will be favourites for the bronze medal.

4 x 100 METRES FREESTYLE RELAY (Women)

Munich 1972		World Championships — Cali 1975	
1. USA	3:55.19	1. GDR	3:49.37
2. GDR	3:55.55	2. USA	3:50.74
3. Ger	3:57.93	3. Can	3:53.37

Diving

Men's springboard World champion Phil Boggs of the US and Italy's Klaus Dibiasi, probably the world's greatest diver, look likely to repeat the contest they had in Cali, which resulted in a narrow win for Boggs. The bronze medal could be won by Strakhov of the USSR, Moore of the US or Munich silver medallist Cagnotto of Italy.

SPRINGBOARD DIVING (Men)

Munich 1972	World Championships — Cali 1975
1. Vladimir Vasin (URS)	1. Philip Boggs (USA)
2. Franco Cagnotto (Ita)	2. Klaus Dibiasi (Ita)
3. Craig Lincoln (USA)	3. Vladimiri Strakhov (URS)

Men's platform Klaus Dibiasi of Italy should have no trouble in winning a remarkable third consecutive Olympic gold medal in this event. Cagnotto of Italy had a poor world championships in Cali but could do well in Montreal along with Mikhailin of the USSR, Giron of Mexico and Vosler of the US.

PLATFORM DIVING (Men)

Munich 1972	World Championships — Cali 1975
1. Klaus Dibiasi (Ita)	1. Klaus Dibiasi (Ita)
2. Richard Rydze (USA)	2. Nikola Milhailin (URS)
3. Franco Cagnotto (Ita)	3. Carlos Ciron (Mex)

Women's springboard The US and Soviet divers are expected to share the medals as they did in Cali. However, one missed or faulty dive can mean the difference between first and sixth place. Ulrika Knape of Sweden could also do well.

Women's platform Sweden's Ulrika Knape, the defending Olympic Champion, could only manage third place in Cali, though it was by a

Below: Christine Loock of the US, who took third place in the springboard diving at the Wold Championships at Cali, 1975.

SPRINGBOARD DIVING (Women)

Munich 1972
1. Micki King (USA)
2. Ulrika Knape (Swe)
3. Marina Janicke (GDR)

World Championships — Cali 1975
1. Irina Kalinina (URS)
2. Tatiana Volynkina (URS)
3. Christine Loock (USA)

PLATFORM DIVING (Women)

Munich 1972
1. Ulrika Knape (Swe)
2. Milena Duchkova (Tch)
3. Marina Janicke (GDR)

World Championships — Cali 1975
1. Janet Ely (USA)
2. Irina Kalinina (URS)
3. Ulrika Knape (Swe)

hundredth of a point. The competition in Montreal looks wide open. The Soviets dived extremely well in Cali and if they repeat that form in Montreal they will be top contenders, together with Janet Ely of the US, the 1975 World Champion.

OLYMPIC SWIMMING RECORDS

MEN

FREESTYLE
100m	51.22	Mark Spitz (USA) 1972
200m	1:52.78	Mark Spitz (USA) 1972
400m	4:00.27	Brad Cooper (Aus) 1972
1,500m	15:52.58	Michael Burton (USA) 1972
4 x 100m	3:26.42	National Team (USA) 1972
		(D. Edgar; J. Murphy; J. Heidenreich; M. Spitz)
4 x 200m	7:35.78	National Team (USA) 1972
		(J. Kinsella; F. Tyler; S. Genter; M. Spitz)

BACKSTROKE
100m	**56.58**	Roland Matthes (GDR) 1972
200m	2:02.82	Roland Matthes (GDR) 1972

BREASTSTROKE
100m	1:04.94	Nobutaka Taguchi (Jpn) 1972
200m	2:21.55	John Hencken (USA) 1972

BUTTERFLY
100m	54.27	Mark Spitz (USA) 1972
200m	2:00.70	Mark Spitz (USA) 1972

MEDLEY
200m	2:07.17	Gunnar Larsson (Swe) 1972
400m	4:31.98	Gunnar Larsson (Swe) 1972
4 x 100m	3:48.16	National Team (USA) 1972
		(M. Stamm; T. Bruce; M. Spitz; J. Heidenreich)

WOMEN

FREESTYLE
100m	58.59	Sandra Neilson (USA) 1972
200m	2:03.56	Shane Gould (Aus) 1972
400m	4:19.04	Shane Gould (Aus) 1972
800m	8:53.68	Keena Rothhammer (USA) 1972
4 x 100m	3:55.19	National Team (USA) 1972
		(S. Neilson; J. Kemp; J. Barkman; S. Babashoff)

BACKSTROKE
100m	1:05.78	Melissa Belote (USA) 1972
200m	2:19.19	Melissa Belote (USA) 1972

BREASTSTROKE
100m	1:13.58	Catherine Carr (USA) 1972
200m	2:41.71	Beverley Whitfield (Aus) 1972

BUTTERFLY
100m	1:03.34	Mayumi Aoki (Jpn) 1972
200m	2:15.57	Karen Moe (USA) 1972

Below: Jim Montgomery of the US
world record holder of the 100m freestyle and
bronze medallist in the 1975 World
Championships, is expected to clash with
teammate Andy Coan in a fight for the gold
at the Olympics.

MEDLEY
200m	2:23.07	Shane Gould (Aus) 1972
400m	5:02.97	Gail Neall (Aus) 1972
4 x 100m	4:20.75	National Team (USA) 1972
		(M. Belote; C. Carr; D. Deardurff; S. Neilson)

WORLD SWIMMING RECORDS
(at distances recognized by the
Fédération Internationale de Natation Amateur)

MEN

FREESTYLE
100m	50.59	James Montgomery (USA) 1975
200m	1:50.32	Bruce Furniss (USA) 1975
400m	3:53.31	Tim Shaw (USA) 1975
800m	8:09.60	Tim Shaw (USA) 1975
1,500m	15:20.91	Tim Shaw (USA) 1975

BREASTSTROKE
100m	1.03.88	John Hencken (USA) 1974
200m	2:18.21	John Hencken (USA) 1974

BUTTERFLY
100m	54.27	Mark Spitz (USA) 1972
200m	2:00.70	Mark Spitz (USA) 1972

BACKSTROKE

100m	56.3*	Roland Matthes (GDR) 1972
100m	56.30†	Roland Matthes (GDR) 1972
200m	2:01.87	Roland Matthes (GDR) 1973

INDIVIDUAL MEDLEY

| 200m | 2:06.08 | Bruce Furniss (USA) 1975 |
| 400m | 4:28.89 | Andras Hargity (Hun) 1974 |

FREESTYLE RELAYS

4 x 100m	3:24.85	United States 1975
		(Bruce Furniss, James Montgomery, Andrew Coan, John Murphy)
4 x 200m	7:33.22	United States 1973
		(Kurt Krumpholz, Robin Backhaus, Richard Klatt, James Montgomery)

MEDLEY RELAY

| 4 x 100m | 3:48.16 | United States 1972 |
| | | (Michael Stamm, Thomas Bruce, Mark Spitz, Jerry Heidenreich) |

*Timed to $\frac{1}{10}$sec
†Achieved in a Medley Race

WOMEN

FREESTYLE

100m	56.22	Kornelia Ender (GDR) 1975
200m	2:02.27	Kornelia Ender (GDR) 1975
400m	4:14.76	Shirley Babashoff (USA) 1975
800m	8:43.48	Jenny Turrall (Aus) 1975
1,500m	16:33.94	Jenny Turrall (Aus) 1974

BREASTSTROKE

| 100m | 1:12.28 | Renate Vogel (GDR) 1974 |
| 200m | 2:34.99 | Karla Linke (GDR) 1974 |

BUTTERFLY

| 100m | 1:01.24 | Kornelia Ender (GDR) 1975 |
| 200m | 2:13.76 | Rosemarie Kother (GDR) 1973 |

BACKSTROKE

| 100m | 1:02.98 | Ulricke Richter (GDR) 1974 |
| 200m | 2:15.46 | Brigit Treiber (GDR) 1975 |

INDIVIDUAL MEDLEY

| 200m | 2:18.83 | Ulrike Tauber (GDR) 1975 |
| 400m | 4:52.20 | Ulrike Tauber (GDR) 1975 |

FREESTYLE RELAY

| 4 x 100m | 3:49.37 | East Germany 1975 |
| | | (Kornelia Ender, Barbara Krause, Claudia Hempel, Ute Bruckner) |

MEDLEY RELAY

| 4 x 100m | 4:13.78 | East Germany 1974 |
| | | (Ulricke Richter, Renate Vogel, Rosemarie Kother, Kornelia Ender) |

COMMONWEALTH SWIMMING RECORDS

MEN

FREESTYLE
100m	52.2*	Michael Wenden (Aus) 1968
	52.22e	Michael Wenden (Aus) 1973
200m	1:53.56	Brian Brinkley (Eng) 1975
400m	3:58.70	Bradford Cooper (Aus) 1973
800m	8:15.02	Stephen Holland (Aus) 1975
1,500m	15:27.79	Stephen Holland (Aus) 1975
4 x 100m	3:33.20	National Team (Can) 1972
		(B. Robertson; B. Phillips; T. Bach; R. Kasting)
4 x 200m	7:42.55	National Team (GBR) 1975
		(A. McClatchey; B. Brinkley; G. Jameson; G. Downie)

BACKSTROKE
100m	57.60	Steve Pickell (Can) 1974
200m	2:05.78	M. Tonelli (Aus) 1975

BREASTSTROKE
100m	1:04.26	David Wilkie (Scot) 1975
200m	2:18.23	David Wilkie (Scot) 1975

BUTTERFLY
100m	55.56	Bruce Robertson (Can) 1972
200m	2:02.47	Brian Brinkley (Eng) 1975

MEDLEY
200m	2:06.32	David Wilkie (Scot) 1974
400m	4:35.70	Jim Fowlie (Can) 1975
4 x 100m	3:52.26	National Team (Can) 1972
		(E. Fish; W. Mahony; B. Robertson; R. Kasting)

WOMEN

FREESTYLE
100m	58.20	Sonya Gray (Aus) 1975
200m	2:03.56	Shane Gould (Aus) 1972
400m	4:17.55	Jenny Turrall (Aus) 1974
800m	8:43.48	Jenny Turrall (Aus) 1975
1,500m	16:33.94	Jenny Turrall (Aus) 1974
4 x 100m	3:53.7	National Team (Can) 1975

BACKSTROKE
100m	1:04.30	Nancy Garapick (Can) 1975
200m	2:16.09	Nancy Garapick (Can) 1975

BREASTSTROKE
100m	1:14.98	Marian Stuart (Can) 1975
200m	2:41.02	Joan Baker (Can) 1975

BUTTERFLY
100m   1:03.88   Barbara Clarke (Can) 1975
200m   2:17.07   Wendy Quirk (Can) 1975

MEDLEY
200m   2:22.07   Becky Smith (Can) 1975
400m   4:58.66   Cheryl Gibson (Can) 1975
4 x 100m   4:24.42   Pt Claire SC (Can) 1975
                        (G. Ladruceur; M. Stuart; W. Quirk; A. Jardin)

*time recorded in $\frac{1}{10}$ second increments
e = record

UK SWIMMING RECORDS
as ratified by the Amateur Swimming Association. Short course and record equalling performances are *not* recognized. Times to only a tenth of a second are manually timed.

MEN

FREESTYLE
100m	53.4	Robert McGregor 1967
200m	1:53.56	Brian Brinkley 1975
400m	4:02.88	Gordon Downie 1975
800m	8:32.13	David Parker 1975
1,500m	15:54.78	James Carter 1974

BREASTSTROKE
100m	1:04.26	David Wilkie 1975
200m	2:18.23	David Wilkie 1975

BUTTERFLY
100m	56.68	Brian Brinkley 1975
200m	2:02.47	Brian Brinkley 1975

BACKSTROKE
100m	59.82	Colin Cunningham 1974
200m	2:08.13	James Carter 1975

INDIVIDUAL MEDLEY
200m	2:06.32	David Wilkie 1974
400m	4:36.29	Brian Brinkley 1973

WOMEN

FREESTYLE
100m	1:00.3	Debbie Hill 1975
200m	2:09.42	Susan Edmondson 1974
400m	4:29.17	Diane Walker 1974
800m	9:17.41	Deborah Simpson 1974
1,500m	18:43.2	Susan Edmondson 1973

BREASTSTROKE
100m	1:15.82	Sandra Dickie 1974
200m	2:42.78	Margaret Kelly 1975

BUTTERFLY
100m	1:05.26	Joanne Atkinson 1975
200m	2:21.15	Joanne Atkinson 1975

BACKSTROKE
100m	1:08.55	Margaret Kelly 1974
200m	2:26.2	Wendy Burrell 1970

INDIVIDUAL MEDLEY
200m	2:25.01	Anne Adams 1975
400m	5:06.71	Susan Richardson 1974

GYMNASTICS

Gold Medallists — Munich 1972

Men

Overall	S Kato (Jpn)
Vault	K Koeste (GDR)
Parallel bars	S Kato (Jpn)
Floor exercises	N Andrianov (URS)
Pommel horse	V Klimenko (URS)
Rings	A Nakayama (Jpn)
Horizontal bar	M Tsukahara (Jpn)
Team	Jpn

Women

Overall	L Turischeva (URS)
Vault	K Janz (GDR)
Asymmetric bars	K Janz (GDR)
Beam	O Korbut ((URS)
Floor exercises	O Korbut (URS)
Team	URS

The 1972 Olympic gymnastics competition was a magnificent spectacle of grace and skill. The agility and strength displayed by both men and women added new dimensions to this, the most aesthetic of sports. Yet the competition is probably best remembered for the tears and joy of a tiny Soviet competitor, Olga Korbut. She wasn't the best gymnast, yet her performance kept hundreds of millions of viewers around the world in suspense. In little over a week she became a world celebrity and gave gymnastics a remarkable boost.

Olga overshadowed — by sheer force of personality — the best woman gymnast at Munich. Ludmilla Turischeva arrived as reigning European and World Overall Champion. She added the Olympic overall gold medal to her list of credits, as well as a team gold medal with the Soviet squad, a silver for the floor exercises and a bronze for the vault. Olga won three golds — the beam, the floor exercises and as a member of the winning Soviet team. The other two golds also went to eastern Europe, with Karin Janz of East Germany winning both the vault and the asymmetric bars.

In the men's gymnastics Sawao Kato led the Japanese team to victory; he was also the overall gold medallist and winner of the parallel bars. His team mates Akinori Nakayama and Mitsuo Tsukahara won the rings and the horizontal bar respectively. The Sovet Union won two golds with Nicolai Andrianov in the floor

exercises and Victor Klimenko on the pommel horse, while Klaus
Koeste of East Germany took the vault.

In the four years that have passed since Munich, gymnastics
competitors have evolved moves of even greater complexity, and the
Montreal Olympics promise to be the best ever. The men will compete
in six exercises, the women in four. Only two exercises are done by
both sexes — the floor exercises and the vault.

The floor exercises are performed on a mat twelve metres square
(approximately forty feet square). The men's exercise lasts one
minute; it must include movements of balance and strength, leaps,
springs, and tumbling movements. The women have one and a half
minutes and perform with musical accompaniment. They must
include leaps, turns, body waves and at least two combinations of
several acrobatic moves. Ballet influenced gymnasts in the 1960s;
today modern dance has added a new dimension of beauty and
interpretation.

The vault involves the same ingredients for men as for women; the
only difference is the position of the horse. For the men it is placed
lengthwise to the run-up, for the women it is across the approach.
The men can place their hands only on the near or the far end of the
horse; the horse is marked and electrically wired to denote any fault in

Left: Zoltan Magyar of Hungary, the supreme
specialist in gymnastics, and undisputed world
champion of the pommel horse. Below: The
great all-round gymnastics champion at the
Munich Games, Ludmilla Turischeva of the
Soviet Union, who joins her immortal
predecessors Latynina and Caslavska.

this respect. The judges look for a long flight on to the horse with the
body at least horizontal, a momentary support with both hands, and a
second flight off the horse to dismount. Steps or hops on landing are
penalized. Each competitor vaults twice, with the best mark counting;
in the finals the competitors must perform two different vaults. Again,
only the best mark counts.

Originally both men and women used the same set-up for the
parallel bars, but after World War II the asymmetric bars were
introduced for women. For men, the bars are at the same height — 5ft
6in; they are 11ft 6in long and the space between the bars can be
adjusted from 1ft 4½in to 1ft 7in. Swing, flight, strength and held
positions must be demonstrated by the men, with at least one point,
above or below the bars, when both hands are released together.

The same apparatus is used for the women's asymmetric bars, with
the lower bar at 4ft 11in and the top one at 7ft 6in. Swinging
movements must predominate, with changes of grasp and direction,
and changes between hanging and supported positions. Both the
men's and the women's exercises last about thirty seconds. If a

gymnast falls from the equipment, he or she is allowed thirty seconds to resume; otherwise the exercise is terminated. A fall is of course penalized.

The last piece of women's apparatus — the beam — is the only piece of equipment not evolved from the men's apparatus. It stands 3ft 11½in off the floor; it is 16ft long and just 4in across the top surface on which the competitor performs. Since Munich, this surface has been covered by chamois leather to give the gymnast greater adhesion. The exercise lasts between 1min 15sec and 1min 35sec and requires a great deal of skill and nerve from the competitor. It is one of the most exciting exercises to watch — turns and pivots, steps, running combinations and acrobatic elements must all be executed without loss of balance on that four inch strip. A fall costs half a mark; after a fall the competitor must continue the exercise within ten seconds or the exercise will be counted as terminated.

The other men's exercises are the pommel horse, the rings and the horizontal bar. The pommel horse stands 3ft 7½in high, with the pommels 16½in apart and 4½in high. The gymnast must execute clean swings, circle his legs both individually and together, and perform both reverse and forward scissors positions. All three zones of the horse must be used, making up a thirty-second non-stop exercise. Penalties are imposed if the legs or any other part of the body touches the horse.

The rings, made of laminated wood, are suspended 8ft 2½in off the floor, from a frame 17ft 6in high. The exercise lasts forty-five seconds

and must contain movements of swing, strength and held positions, including at least two handstands and one of the more difficult maintained positions. Penalties are imposed if there is too much swing on the suspension cords, if the feet are used to balance, or if the balances are not held long enough.

Finally, there is the most exciting men's exercise — the horizontal bar. The exercise is performed on a steel bar 8ft 2½in off the floor, around which the gymnast executes a non-stop combination of swings, complete circles with variations and links, and changes of hand grasp. The judges look for good extension on the swings, and a good finish, including the dismount and landing. Some gymnasts are now trying triple somersaults as they dismount!

Marking these exercises are four judges and a head judge, who becomes involved only if the difference between the four judges' marks is too great. Of the four judges' marks, the highest and lowest are discarded and the other two are averaged to give the competitor's score.

All competitors – there were a hundred and thirteen men and a hundred and eighteen women in Munich — take part in set and voluntary exercises on each piece of equipment. Then the top thirty-six go forward to another set of voluntary exercises, to decide the overall Olympic gold medallist.

Each country is allowed a maximum of six competitors; the five marked highest total their score to give the team result. For the apparatus finals, the six highest competitors on each item of

apparatus in the overall competition go forward to compete again to decide the gold medallist for each apparatus.

Who will win in Montreal? One should be able to stick one's neck out and say that the Japanese men and the Soviet women will win the team gold medals, and it is most likely that a Japanese man will win the overall gold medal. Favourite will be Shigeru Kasamatsu, the 1974 World Champion and winner of the vault and floor. He leads a team which includes Eizo Kenmotsu, World Champion on parallel bars; Hiroshi Kajiyama, runner up in the 1975 World Cup at Wembley and winner of the floor in that event, and Mitsuo Tsukahara, World Cup gold medallist on rings and high bar.

Main challenger to Japanese overall supremacy will be Nicolai Andrianov, the Soviet winner of the 1975 World Cup and silver medallist overall in the 1975 World Championship. Andrianov is also World Champion on rings, and another East European — Zoltan Magyar of Hungary — is World Champion and World Cup winner on the pommel horse. The only west European to hold a world title is Eberhard Gienger from West Germany, who won the horizontal bar in 1974.

Picking a women's overall gold medallist poses the greatest problem. Ludmilla Turischeva will be there and despite her remarkable comeback in the 1975 World Cup, when she swept the board with the overall championship, as well as all the individual apparatus championships, this highly respected Soviet gymnast will be seriously challenged by Olga Korbut (who was off form in the 1975 World Cup) as well as by five girls who did not take part in the World Cup. Foremost among these five is fourteen-year-old Nadia Comanechi of Rumania, who made a stunning rise to fame in April 1975 when she won 'Champions All', an international invitational meet at Wembley, England. Three weeks later she became overall European Champion at Skien in Norway, completely eclipsing Turischeva and winning individual championships in the vault, beam and asymmetric bars. To cap a remarkable six months, she went to Montreal and won the pre-Olympic tournament! Among her strongest opponents at the Olympics will be a new Soviet star, Nellie Kim, who beat Ludmilla Turischeva in the Soviet Games, and four East German girls — Annelore Zinke, Richarda Schmeisser, Gitta Escher, and Angelika Hellman. If Nadia Comanechi can sustain the brilliant form she showed through 1975, her battle with the Soviet and East German stars should be the highlight of the Olympic gymnastics competition.

WEIGHTLIFTING

Gold Medallists — Munich 1972		Total kg	lb
Flyweight	Z Smalcerz (Pol)	337.5	743¾
Bantamweight	I Foeldi (Hun)	377.5	831¾
Featherweight	N Nurikyan (Bul)	402.5	887
Lightweight	M Kirzhinov (URS)	460.0	1013¾
Middleweight	Y Bikov (Bul)	485.0	1068¾
Light heavyweight	L Jensen (Ncr)	507.5	1118½
Middle heavyweight	A Nikolov (Bul)	525.0	1157
Heavyweight	U Talts (URS)	580.0	1278¼
Super heavyweight	V Alexeyev (URS)	640.0	1410¾

The eastern European and Soviet countries, who won eight of the nine gold medals at Munich, are expected to strengthen their grip on weightlifting in the 1976 Olympics, when there will be contests in nine categories, ranging from flyweight (under 114lb) to super

heavyweight (over 242½lb). Although the clean and press, in which the
bar is pressed evenly overhead, has been eliminated from the event
because of refereeing difficulties, this is not expected to bring about
great changes in the results. With advantages in facilities and
coaching, the Soviets and eastern Europeans have increased their
lead over the rest of the world on the two remaining lifts, the snatch
and the clean and jerk — the best efforts on each are aggregated to
give the competitor his total poundage.

In the 1975 World Championships in Moscow only one medal out of
twenty-seven was secured by a representative from a non-communist
country. The USSR, who took over the leadership of the sport from
the USA during the 1950s, took the team title in the 1975
Championships, but they have recently had their domination shaken
by the Bulgarians, who have revolutionized weightlifting by instituting
twice-daily training. It was previously considered that forty-eight
hours should elapse between heavy training sessions to allow the
body to recover.

The most successful — and famous — Soviet lifter is super
heavyweight Vasily Alexeyev, a 350lb mining engineer, who has been
undefeated since taking his first world title in 1970. The thirty-three-
year old Alexeyev, who enjoys a whole leg of lamb and a mixed grill
for lunch, may have to lift nearly 550lb overhead in the clean and jerk
to defeat his two principal rivals, East German Gerd Bonk and
Bulgarian Khristo Plachkov, in the Montreal Olympics. Bonk finished
only 11lb behind Alexeyev in the clean and jerk at the 1975 World
Championships while Plachkov, who set a world record of 429½lb in
the snatch, nearly fixed 440¾lb in the clean and jerk.

Another opponent who could challenge Alexeyev's title of 'the
world's strongest man' is Bulgaria's nineteen-year-old Valentin
Khristov, who took the heavyweight crown in 1975 with 920¾lb, only
22lb below Alexeyev. He may put on more bodyweight before the
Montreal Olympics and thus become a contender in Alexeyev's super
heavyweight class.

World middle heavyweight title holder is David Rigert of the USSR,
who will want to make amends for his Munich performance when,
after missing all his snatches, he was eliminated from the competition
and went berserk in his bedroom, smashing his head against the wall.
He was forcibly given sedatives before being sent back to the USSR.
He may well redeem his pride by winning the middle heavyweight
class in Montreal.

JUDO

The perennial question in judo is: 'How many titles will the Japanese win?' As inventors of the sport — and still the dominant force — they regarded their performance at the Munich Olympics as a disgrace. They won only three gold medals!

At the 1975 World Championships they lost two titles and were fortunate not to lose two more, partly because they ignored the services of Isao Okano, the trainer who had inspired them to take all six gold medals at the 1973 World Championships. If Okano is

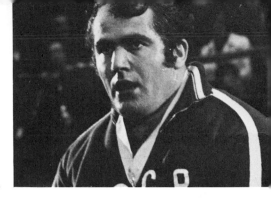

Below left: Great Britain's silver medallist team in judo in the European Championships, 1974, which included Olympic silver medallist Dave Starbrook (second from left) and bronze medallist Brian Jacks (third from left). Right: Onashvili of the Soviet Union, a bronze medallist in judo at the Munich Olympics who has since taken the European heavyweight title at Crystal Palace in 1975.

restored to his position then the Japanese may recover some of their prestige.

At Montreal judo contestants will again be competing in five weight classes and an open (unlimited weight) class. At the Olympics, pressure is greater on individual fighters because countries are allowed to enter only one competitor per class, as opposed to two competitors per class at world championships.

The advance of nations like Britain, the USSR, East Germany, Korea, and France will ensure that the Japanese will have a struggle in every class. The USSR has two top competitors, Sergei Novikov, who lost the 1975 world heavyweight title to Japan's Sumio Endo only because of a refereeing mistake, and Shota Chochoshvili, the 1972 Olympic light heavyweight champion, who will be awkward to defeat in the open class.

France's Jean-Luc Rouge is the reigning World Champion in the light heavyweight division. His chief opponents will include Britain's Dave Starbrook, the 1972 Olympic silver medallist, whose training includes daily runs round London's Regent Park in army boots, and East Germany's Dietmar Lorenz, the current European champion.

Japan's outstanding prospect is Shozo Fujii, who is three-time World Champion in the middleweight class. He is likely to face stern opposition from men like France's Jean-Paul Coche and Britain's Brian Jacks, both of whom took bronze medals in Munich. Fujii's arm strength — he climbs up ropes one-handed — and suppleness enable him to uproot even the most stable of opponents with his shoulder throw, in which he hurls competitors over his own back to the mat.

The Japanese are traditionally best in the lighter classes and although Yoshiharu Minami is favourite for the lightweights Vladimir Nevzorov of the USSR became the first non-Japanese ever to take the world title in the welterweight class in Vienna, 1975.

A major influence on the results will be the draw. There is no seeding and the event — one category per day — is run on a knock-out basis. Although there is a repechage, no competitor who suffers an unlucky defeat can reach the final.

BOXING

Olympic boxing has expanded from the seven weight divisions introduced at St Louis in 1904, to the eleven introduced at Mexico in 1968. The US had a clean sweep in St Louis, but managed only one gold medallist at Munich in 1972.

A country can enter only one competitor at each weight. The light flyweight division (105lb, 47.627kg) was introduced specifically to foster enthusiasm in the countries of the Far East. But a Venezuelan and a Hungarian were the first winners.

Olympic boxing is totally controlled by the Association Internationale de Boxe Amateur (AIBA) which was begun by London solicitor Rudyard Russell, who was president until 1975. The European bloc of the AIBA is now headed by Hoffman of the Netherlands. The AIBA, with a selected panel of referees and judges, all trial tested, and a stringent medical commission, stage the biennial European championships. Their code of officiating is now accepted in all parts of the world.

There is no qualifying standard for Olympic boxing, and too many countries enter boxers who are not prepared for the toughness of the competition. The AIBA are now considering staging an eliminating series to cut down the number of entries before Olympic competition begins.

The boxers at the top of the Olympic competition are usually regulars on the international circuit. For many of them, a gold medal is the quickest route to professional big-money fights, and even those who never reach the winner's rostrum at the Olympics may become professional champions. At 18, Mohammed Ali proved a potential

Previous page: The outstanding boxer at any
weight in the Munich Olympics and since
then at world championships and Pan Am
Games is undoubtedly Teofilo Stevenson of
Cuba, who has resisted all attempts by US
entrepreneurs to turn him professional.

world beater at the Rome Olympics in 1960. He won the light heavyweight gold, eliminating pro-style Australian, Tony Madigan, plus the pick of the USSR and Poland.

The state-aided Cubans produced the stars at the Munich Olympics. Heavyweight gold medallist Teofilo Stevenson was hailed around the world as another Ali in the making. Stevenson subsequently lost a bout in Cuba against Ion Alexe of Rumania who had been ruled out of the Munich final with a broken thumb. However, he came back strongly to win in the Pan American Games and could again be favourite at Montreal.

Cuba also staged the first unofficial world amateur championships in 1974 to show their prowess, but not all countries entered.

To stem the controversy created by the use of five judges, the AIBA has introduced white-tipped gloves, to help judges determine whether blows have been correctly delivered. For example, 'slapping' blows, which are often spectacular from a rear seat, should not be scored. A knockdown, according to the AIBA, should not be marked with a higher score than a correctly delivered blow that does not put a boxer down. The emphasis must be on style and defence.

A great deal depends upon the draw in Olympic boxing, as two favourites can be matched in the first series. But, in spite of the occasional 'controversial' verdict, it is usually the best boxers who win the gold.

ROWING

Gold Medallists — 1972 Olympics

Coxed fours	West Germany
Coxless pairs	East Germany
Single sculls	Yuri Malischev (URS)
Coxed pairs	East Germany
Coxless fours	East Germany
Double sculls	USSR
Eight	New Zealand

Rowers will be competing for a total of fourteen gold medals and Olympic titles in Montreal. Eight Olympic titles will be in the men's heavyweight events, divided into five rowing and three sculling

events. The rowing events are the eights, the coxed and coxless fours and the coxed and coxless pairs. The men's sculling events consist of the single and double sculls and the quadruple sculls — a new event introduced in 1974.

For the first time ever women's rowing will be introduced to the Olympic programme in Montreal. The six women's inaugural Olympic titles will be in the eights, the coxed fours, the coxless pairs and three sculling events — the single and double sculls, and the quadruple sculls with coxswain.

In the men's events racing will be over 2,000 metres; the women will compete over 1000 metres. In the rowing and sculling championships, a crew has to fail twice in order to be eliminated from the competition. Crews failing to qualify for the semi-finals or the finals have a last opportunity in the repechages — where the racing and tempo of the competition really picks up.

The theme for the 1976 Olympic Regatta in Montreal will be a simple one — East Germany versus the world. The East Germans dominate rowing more than any other country commands any other sport. Since East Germany gained their sporting independence in 1966, the men have captured no less than thirty-two gold medals in Olympic, World and European Regattas. (Next in the medal tables over the same period are the Soviet Union and West Germany with eight titles apiece). In the 1975 World Championships in Nottingham, the East German oarsmen and scullers captured five of the eight titles and took a medal in the other three events. In the same championships the East German oarswomen took five of the six gold medals.

The two prestige events of the Olympic Regatta are the eights, 'the blue riband of the sport', and the single sculls — 'the race for the loners'. In the eights the eastern bloc threat will come from East Germany and the Soviet Union. But a considerable challenge will be expected from the English-speaking nations. New Zealand, holders of the Olympic title, may lead the challenge, along with the 1974 World Champions, the US. The dark horse will be Great Britain, who won the silver medal in the 1974 World Championships. Australia, who reached the 1975 World Championship final, and West Germany could also be strong contenders.

The favourite for the single sculls title will be the twenty-two-year-old world champion Peter-Michael Kolbe of West Germany. His main threats will be from the strong twenty-nine-year-old Irishman, Sean

Drea, and from either Martin Winter or Wolfgang Hönig of East Germany. The dark horse in this event could be the tall Finn, Pertti Karpinnen, or Ibarra of Argentina.

East Germany will start favourites in the coxed and coxless pairs, the quadruple sculls and the coxless fours. They will be strongly challenged in the double sculls by the Hansen brothers of Norway and by Britain's Mike Hart and Chris Baillieu. The USSR will start favourites for the coxed fours with their world champion 'Polar Bears' coxed four. In the women's events, the East German eights should be closely pressed by the United States. But the East Germans look destined for a medal in all fourteen rowing and sculling events and many of them will be gold.

CANOEING

Gold Medallists — 1972 Olympics

Men

Kayak (single)	U Shaparenko (URS)
Kayak (pairs)	USSR
Canoe (single)	I Patzaichin (Rom)
Canoe (pairs)	USSR
Kayak (fours)	USSR

Women

Kayak (single)	Y Ryabchinskaya (URS)
Kayak (pairs)	USSR

Sadly the eye-catching 'white water' slalom events are omitted for the 1976 Olympic Games, leaving canoeing to the traditional still-water sprint canoeists.

The Olympic canoeing programme has been increased from seven to eleven events. The established events are the men's kayak single, kayak double, kayak fours, canoe single, and canoe double which are all run over 1,000 metres, together with two women's events — the kayak single and kayak double, run over 500 metres. The new events for Montreal are men's events run over 500 metres — kayak single, kayak double, canoe single and canoe double.

At the 1975 World Championships in Belgrade eastern European

dominance of canoeing was broken, with Spain, Norway and Italy among the surprising gold medal winners in the men's events. Since Munich, the Soviet Union have been suspiciously low in profile and many predict they will emerge once again in Montreal. The East German women canoeists are dominant in the two kayak events. Britain's main hope for a medal lies with twenty-three-year-old physical education student Douglas Parnham, who has reached the final round in the men's kayak single over 500 metres in the last three world championships.

Canada, too, have medal hopes in John Wood in the Canadian single and in Olympic skier Sue Holloway — a kayak specialist. These two, however, may opt for the double title with Wood taking Greg Smith on board and Sue Holloway partnering Caron Tippett.

The top Australian and New Zealand canoeists have not been seen in Europe since Munich and will therefore be regarded as outsiders for final and medal chances.

YACHTING

Gold Medallists — 1972 Olympics

Finn Class	Serge Maury (Fra)
Flying Dutchman	Rodney Pattison (GBR)
Tempest	Valentin Mankin (URS)
Soling	Harry (Bud) Melges (USA)
Star	David Forbes (Aus)
Dragon	John Cuneo (Aus)

The Yachting Olympics will be held at Kingston on Lake Ontario, about 160 miles from Montreal. Six different classes of boat will compete, each class having a series of seven races on a point-scoring basis to determine the overall positions and medals. The final scoring for each boat will be based on the best six out of seven races, thus discarding the worst result of the series (to allow for accidents or gear failure).

The six classes in yachting are:
Finn Class (single-handed dinghy)
Flying Dutchman (two-man dinghy)
Tempest (two-man keel boat)
Soling (three-man keel boat)
470 Dinghy (two-man dinghy)
Tornado Catamaran (two-man twin hull)

The 470 Dinghy and the Tornado Catamaran replace the outdated Star and Dragon classes of boat. Kingston will witness for the first time in a yachting Olympics the catamaran or twin-hulled boat.

In many classes of boats, national selection will be more difficult than winning in the Olympics. An example of this is the case of Reg White and Ian Fraser of Great Britain in the Tornados. Both are outstanding competitors, but only one can catch the selectors' eyes.

Britain's Rodney Pattison must start favourite for his third successive Olympic gold medal in the Flying Dutchman, and naval officer David Howlett will hope to repeat the first place he gained in the 1975 pre-Olympic regatta at Kingston in the single-handed Finn. Strongly favoured for a medal in the new 470 class are either of the Frenchmen, Jean-Louis Guyader or Marc Laurent, with other continental boats prominent.

Leading Commonwealth hopes include Jock Bilger (New Zealand) who gained second place in the Flying Dutchman 1975 World Championships; John Bertrand (Australia), second to David Howlett in the Finn class in the Kingston 1975 pre-Olympic regatta; David Forbes (Australia), Olympic holder of the discontinued Star class now concentrating on the Soling boat; and Hans Fogh (Canada), a leading world competitor with considerable experience in the Flying Dutchman.

EQUESTRIAN

The three day event is divided into dressage, a tough cross-country ride and a final showjumping course. The British have traditionally been strong contenders — they have won the team gold medal three times in the last twenty years and are expected to make a good showing in Montreal, where they are likely to be led by Richard Meade, individual three day champion at Munich. Other strong possibilities for the British team are Lucinda Prior-Palmer, winner of the European Championship, Princess Anne, who was runner-up, and her husband Capt. Mark Phillips, who rode brilliantly into second place at Burghley.

The Canadians seem likely to pose a major challenge to British supremacy at the three day event. They took the team gold medal in the 1975 pre-Olympic competition and the silver medal behind the US in the 1975 Pan American Games, with a team which included Peter

Howard, Elizabeth Ashton, Jim Day and Jim Henry. However, the US also poses a strong threat with World Champion Bruce Davidson, and a good showing is expected from the USSR.

In showjumping West Germany are firm favourites for gold medals, with such stars as world champion Hartwig Stecken, and European champion Alwin Schokemohle. However, the Canadians may be hard to beat with such riders as Jim Day, Jimmy Elder, Norma Chornawaka, and Ian Miller. Although they had a disappointing showing at the Pan American Games, mainly through lack of fit horses, the Canadians have a fine record — including the team gold medal for showjumping in the 1968 Olympics — and are expected to make a strong showing on their home ground. Australian show-jumper Kevin Bacon did well in the 1975 New York Show and should figure prominently in the Olympics, as should the US team. British showjumping stars David Broome and Harvey Smith will be unable to compete because they have complied with International Equestrian Federation requirements and are therefore registered as professionals.

In dressage, horse and rider must perform a demanding series of movements, in which they are marked for control and style. Continental teams usually lead in this highly specialized form of riding and the West Germans and Soviets must be considered favourites to take the dressage medals, though British standards have recently risen considerably.

CYCLING

Gold Medallists — 1972 Olympics

Sprint	D Morelon (Fra)
Tandem sprint	USSR
Individual pursuit, 4,000m	K Knudsen (Nor)
Team pursuit, 4,000m	West Germany
Time trial, 1,000m	N Fredborg (Den)
Team time trial, 100km	USSR
Individual road race, 200km	H Kuiper (Hol)

It is unusual for a cyclist to gain gold medals in two separate Olympics, but Frenchman Daniel Morelon achieved just that when he won the individual sprint event in both Mexico and Munich. He'll be

back again in Montreal, going for his third title.

The individual sprint always provides a great tactical battle as it is the man in the back position who is better placed; he can watch every move up front and get in his opponent's 'slipstream', which gives him an easier ride. Trying to manoeuvre the other man to the front is part of the mental and physical battle; it produces the very slow start common to all sprint contests. The tandem sprint, run on a similar basis, has now been excluded from Olympic competition.

The kilometre, or 1,000 metre time trial, is a track event in which each man makes his attempt alone and unpaced, running against the clock. The results are sometimes so close that they must be taken to a thousandth of a second. The pursuit events, both individual and team over 4,000 metres, also require timing. In both events the contestants set off on opposite sides of the track, to try to catch their opponent(s). When things are evenly balanced it is the man or men with the fastest time for the distance who are declared the winners.

There are two road events, the 100 kilometre team time trial and the individual road race, held over 110 miles. In the individual road race, the winner is always unpredictable. The battle for gold in the team race is expected to be between the current world champions, Poland, and the Munich champions, the USSR.

Britain's best hope is in the 4,000 metre team pursuit, in which they won a bronze medal in Munich. Precision and timing as well as strength are needed and with the right team combination they could beat the West German favourites.

Canada has a great chance in the kilometre with Jocelyn Lovell, who made a fine fifth place finish in the 1975 world title contest. He will have strong competition from East Germany and the USSR, who are favourites in both the kilometre and the individual pursuit. However, cycling is a sport in which upsets are traditional and the Montreal Olympics promise some exciting races.

FIELD HOCKEY

Munich 1972

1. West Germany
2. Pakistan
3. India
4. Holland
5. Australia
6. Great Britain

For the first time in Olympic history only twelve countries will be represented in Montreal, instead of sixteen as in the past. The tournament will be played on artificial turf pitches and the sides will be in two groups of six, the winners of Group A playing the runners-up of Group B and vice versa in the semi-finals.

At Munich in 1972, West Germany beat Pakistan 1-0 in the final to win the gold medal and India beat Holland 3-1 in the play-off for the bronze. These four countries are automatically invited to the 1976 Games, as is Canada, the host nation. Argentina, winners at the Pan American Games, have qualified and so have Australia, who will represent the antipodes after beating New Zealand in a play-off. A winner will emerge from the Pan African Games, possibly Ghana or Kenya, and there are several strong reasons for Malaysia to be selected after their splendid performance in the 1975 World Cup, which was won by India with Pakistan runners-up, West Germany third, Malaysia fourth, Australia fifth, and Great Britain sixth. Belgium, France, Poland, the USSR and Spain are all rated as major hockey nations and have a claim to be considered. The British, who started the game, will be bitterly disappointed if they are not included. We must assume they will be, in spite of their rather indifferent performances in recent years, but it is nearly a quarter of a century since they won an Olympic medal in field hockey.

The standard of field hockey throughout the world has never been higher. The game has become almost professional in outlook and there are several exciting players to look out for from the leading countries.

On the Indian team, the attack revolves round inside forward Ashok Kumar, the son of Dyhan Chand, father-figure of Indian hockey and probably the greatest centre forward in the game's history. The present centre forward is speedy Govinda and at the heart of the defence there are two outstanding players, Michael Kindo at full back, and Ajitpal Singh, one of the best centre halves in the world.

The captain of Pakistan's team, Abdul Rashid, is a prolific goal-scoring forward, and he has two brilliant wingers in Samiullah and Islahuddin. Manzoor is a powerful, highly experienced back who scores regularly from penalty corners by the judicious use of vicious undercutting.

The West German team have retained most of their Munich gold medallists including Wolfgang Rott, the goalkeeper, Michael Peter, the best sweeper in the game, Michael Krause, a penalty corner

expert, Horst Drose, an inside forward or midfield player with marvellous stickwork and ball control, and Peter Trump, a strong, fast left winger.

Holland were world champions in 1973 but since then they have been rebuilding, following the retirement of the Spitz brothers and Zweerts. Their preparations have not been helped by the leg injuries suffered by Theo Kruize in a car accident.

Great Britain's team must be classed as an outsider but it will include many fine players, the most accomplished being Rui Saldanha, the centre half, who came to England from Kenya and whose stickwork is just as good as that of the Indians and Pakistanis. The strong man in defence is Paul Svehlik who shares the penalty corner striking with Steve Long from Suffolk, a goal-poaching forward who scored all five goals for England against Ireland in 1974. Bernie Cotton, the captain, is a tremendous competitor, and Ian Thomson, from the Hounslow club, the most promising young player.

Prior to Munich, I predicted that the gold, silver and bronze medals would be shared between West Germany, India and Pakistan. I have seen nothing since to alter my forecast for 1976, particularly as West Germany beat Pakistan 3-2 in the pre-Olympic tournament final in Montreal last year. (India did not take part.) However, Holland, Great Britain or Australia may challenge the supremacy of these three and come through as surprise medallists in Montreal.

MODERN PENTATHLON

1972 Olympics		*World Championships 1975*	
1. A Balczo (Hun)	5412 pts	P Lednev (URS)	5056
2. B Onischenko (URS)	5335	I Kancsal (Hun)	5025
3. P Lednev (URS)	5328	J Fox (GBR)	5016
4. J Fox (GBR)	5311	T Marackso (Hun)	4924
5. V Schmelev (URS)	5302	V Shmelev (URS)	4889
6. B Ferm (Swe)	5283	B Lager (Swe)	4875
Team Result		Team Result	
1) USSR 2) Hungary 3) Finland		1) Hungary 2) USA 3) USSR 4) GB	

Unlike the decathlon and pentathlon in track and field athletics, the five distinct disciplines of the modern pentathlon are designed for

contrast, demanding not only strength and stamina but skill, touch and accuracy. No sport remains more in line with its original Greek forerunner, for it has always been the supreme test of the all-round athlete.

Consider the versatility required in the five day event. All competitors must a) ride an unknown horse over a course of 1,000 metres and 20 fences, b) fence with an épée against all other competitors (59 in Munich!), c) take 20 pistol shots at a snap target from 25 metres range, d) swim 300 metres against the clock, and e) run 4,000 metres over a tough cross-country course. The modern pentathlon was introduced to the Olympic programme in 1912 and until 1960 it was dominated by Sweden. Since then Hungary have taken over in close competition with the USSR. At Munich the Budapest mechanic, Andras Balczo, won his first Olympic gold medal after being five-time world champion and runner-up in Mexico by a single point. If his was one of the most deserving gold medals of all time, so was the third place in the 1975 world championships won by Britain's Sgt Jim Fox. In the view of many he was 'robbed' of a medal in Munich and he had to be given oxygen following his run in Mexico City's altitude in the world championships. For more than a decade he has been Britain's supreme all-rounder and he carries the hopes of many in Montreal.